T0295863

Enforcement of International Environmental Law

The international community has generated several hundred multilateral environmental agreements, yet it has been far less successful in developing means to ensure that contracting parties honour them in practice. The subject of law enforcement has traditionally attracted relatively little attention amongst international policy-makers at the formation stage of a multilateral environmental accord. Commonly, the question of how to secure collective adherence to environmental treaty regimes might well only be considered in depth at a much later stage of an environmental agreement's evolution, if at all. At the same time, the significance of the issue of enforcement has gradually received more considered attention by states and international institutions. Providing an analysis of the nature, extent and current state of the international legal framework concerned with enhancing effective implementation of international environmental law, this book considers the scope and impact of international rules of law whose remit is to require or promote compliance by states with their international environmental legal obligations.

Dr Martin Hedemann-Robinson is a Senior Lecturer in Law at the University of Kent, UK, and a former legal administrator of the European Commission.

Routledge Research in International Environmental Law

The Precautionary Principle in Marine Environmental Law
With Special Reference to High Risk Vessels
Bénédicte Sage-Fuller

International Environmental Law and Distributive Justice
The Equitable Distribution of CDM Projects under the Kyoto Protocol
Tomilola Akanle Eni-Ibukun

Environmental Governance in Europe and Asia
A Comparative Study of Institutional and Legislative Frameworks
Jona Razzaque

Climate Change, Forests and REDD
Lessons for Institutional Design
Edited by Joyeeta Gupta, Nicolien van der Grijp and Onno Kuik

International Environmental Law and the Conservation of Coral Reefs
Edward J. Goodwin

International Environmental Law and the International Court of Justice
Aleksandra Cavoski

Enforcement of International Environmental Law
Challenges and Responses at the International Level
Martin Hedemann-Robinson

https://www.routledge.com/Routledge-Research-in-International-Environmental-Law/book-series/INTENVLAW

Enforcement of International Environmental Law

Challenges and Responses at the International Level

Martin Hedemann-Robinson

LONDON AND NEW YORK

First published 2019
by Routledge
2 Park Square, Milton Park, Abingdon, Oxon OX14 4RN

and by Routledge
711 Third Avenue, New York, NY 10017

Routledge is an imprint of the Taylor & Francis Group, an informa business

British Library Cataloguing in Publication Data
A catalogue record for this book is available from the British Library

Library of Congress Cataloging in Publication Data
Names: Hedemann-Robinson, Martin, author.
Title: Enforcement of international environmental law : challenges and responses at the international level / Martin Hedemann-Robinson.
Description: Abingdon, Oxon ; New York, NY : Routledge, 2018. | Series: Routledge research in international environmental law | Includes bibliographical references and index.
Identifiers: LCCN 2018018805 | ISBN 9781138479104 (hbk)
Subjects: LCSH: Environmental law, International. | Law enforcement.
Classification: LCC K3585 .H43 2018 | DDC 344.04/6–dc23 LC record available at https://lccn.loc.gov/2018018805

ISBN: 978-1-138-47910-4 (hbk)
ISBN: 978-1-351-06658-7 (ebk)

Typeset in Times New Roman
by Taylor & Francis Books

Contents

Preface

One of the greatest challenges confronting contemporary International Environmental Law concerns the need to address widespread failures on the part of several nation states to ensure its proper implementation. Whilst the international community has generated several hundred international agreements intended to protect the environment, it has, however, been far less successful in developing means to ensure that contracting parties honour these accords in practice.

The issue of law enforcement, whilst crucial for the long-term credibility of international environmental law, has traditionally attracted relatively little attention amongst international policy-makers at the formation stage of a multilateral environmental accord. Commonly, the question of how to secure collective adherence to an international environmental agreement might well only be considered in depth at a relatively late stage of treaty negotiations, and sometimes it has not been specifically addressed at all. At the same time, it is fair to say that the significance of the issue of enforcement has gradually received more considered attention by states and international institutions alike. This book considers the contribution made by international legal principles and treaty initiatives intended to enhance states' compliance with their international environmental obligations. Particular attention is paid to the role played by certain collective review systems, incorporated within the fabric of a number of international environmental agreement regimes since the 1990s, to address non-compliance matters. In addition, a few international environmental agreements contain sanctioning mechanisms which may be used as a means of steering defaulting contracting parties back onto the path of compliance. However, sanctions regimes remain rare at international level.

For the most part, concerns over potential or actual loss of national sovereignty have influenced several states in the context of appraising the need for more effective systems to ensure that International

Environmental Law is properly implemented and enforced at national level. Most states appear to remain reluctant to accept the idea of establishing and developing international-level systems endowed with effective supervisory powers for the purpose of overseeing implementation of international environmental treaty obligations. Instead, most remain wedded to the traditional intergovernmentalist approach of deference to individual states over implementation matters within their respective domestic territories. The European Union constitutes a notable exception on the international plane in this regard, its constituent member states having agreed to create and vest supranational institutions (administrative and judicial) with meaningful supervisory as well as sanctioning powers for the purpose of assisting in ensuring that Union obligations, including environmental protection commitments, are properly implemented at national level. Whether the EU continues to be an exceptional case remains to be seen, although it might be argued that international support in supranational governance continues to wane (given not least recent events such as the UK's referendum 2016 vote in favour of Brexit and the current US federal government's faith in mercantilist methods for addressing trade issues). What does remain clear is that due implementation and enforcement of International Environmental Law will continue to face significant hurdles and challenges if individual states are left alone to ensure fulfilment of their international environmental obligations, effectively given the responsibility to mark their own homework.

Table of cases

International Court of Justice

Australia v France (Interim Protection) (1973) ICJ Reports 99; (Judgment) (1974) ICJ Reports 253
New Zealand v France (Interim Protection) (1973) ICJ Reports 135; (Judgment) (1974) ICJ Reports 457
Fisheries Jurisdiction (UK v Norway) (1974) ICJ Reports 116
Barcelona Traction, Light and power Company Ltd (Second Application) (Belgium v Spain) (1970) ICJ Reports 1
Advisory Opinion of the ICJ on Legality of the Threat or Use of Nuclear Weapons [1996] ICJ Reports 226
Gabcikovo-Nagymaros (Hungary v Slovakia) (1997) ICJ Reports 7
Estai Case (Canada v Spain) [1998] ICJ Reports 432
Pulp Mills on the River Uruguay (Argentina v Uruguay) (2010) ICJ Reports 18
Aerial Herbicide Spraying (Ecuador v Columbia) [2013] ICJ Reports 278

International Tribunal for the Law of the Sea

The MOX Plant Case (Provisional Measures) (Ireland v UK) ITLOS (2002) 41 ILM 405
Southern Blue Fin Tuna (Australia and New Zealand v Japan) (2000) 39 ILM 1359

International Arbitral Decisions

Behring Sea Fur Seals Fisheries Arbitration (UK v US) [1898] 1 *Moore's International Arbitration Awards* 755
Trail Smelter Arbitration (US v Canada) (1941) RIAA 1907

Lac Lanoux Arbitration (Spain v France) (1957) 24 ILR 101
Iron Rhine Arbitration (Belgium v Netherlands) (2005) PCA (Case 2003–02)
MOX Plant Arbitration (Jurisdiction and Provisional Measures) (*Ireland v UK*) PCA (2008) (Case 2002–01)

Court of Justice of the EU

Case 25/62 *Plaumann v Commission* [1963] ECR 95
Case 147/78 *France v UK* [1979] ECR I-225
Case C-387/97 *Commission v Greece (Kouroupitos landfill (2))* [1999] ECR I-3257
Case C-278/01 *Commission v Spain (Bathing Waters (2))* [2003] ECR I-14141
Case C-304/02 *Commission v France (Fishing Controls (2))* [2005] ECR I-6263
Case C-459/03 *Commission v Ireland* [2006] ECR I-4635
Case C-237/07 *Janecek v Bavaria* [2008] ECR I-6211
Case C-121/07 *Commission v France (GMO Controls (2))* [2008] ECR I-9195
Case C-279/11 *Commission v Ireland (EIA (2))* EU:C:2012:834
Case C-374/11 *Commission v Ireland (Waste Water Treatment Systems (2))* EU:C:2012:827
C-583/11P *Inuit Tapiriit Kanatami and Others* EU:C:2013:625
Case C-533/11 *Commission v Belgium (Waste Water Treatment Systems (2))* EU:C:2013:659
Case C-576/11*Commission v Luxembourg (Waste Water Treatment Systems (2))* EU:C:2013:773
Case C-196/13 *Commission v Italy* (*Italian Illegal Landfills (2))* EU:C:2014:2407
Case C-378/13 *Commission v Greece* (*Greek Illegal Landfills (2))* EU:C:2014:2405
Case C-243/13 *Commission v Sweden* (*Swedish IPPC (2))* EU:C:2014:2413
Cases C-401–403/12P *Council, EP and Commission v Vereniging Milieudefensie and Stichting Stop Luchtverontreiniging Utrecht*, EU:C:2015:4
Case C-653/13*Commission v Italy (Campania Waste (2))* EU:C:2015:478
Case C-167/14 *Commission v Greece* (*Greek Urban Wastewater (2))* EU:C:2015:684
Case C-557/14 *Commission v Portugal (Portuguese Urban Wastewater (2))* EU:C:2016:471

Case C-584/14 *Commission v Greece* (*Greek Hazardous Waste Planning (2))* EU:C:2016:636
Case C-441/17R *Commission v Poland (Puszcza Białowieska Nature Site)* EU:C:2017:877
Case C-328/16 *Commission v Greece (Thriasio Pedio Wastewater (2))* EU:C:2018:98

Table of treaties and environmental legislation

International treaties

1946 International Convention for the Regulation of Whaling (161 U. N.T.S.72)
1960 Paris OECD Convention on Third Party Liability in the Field of Nuclear Energy (956 U.N.T.S. 251)
1963 IAEA Vienna Convention on Civil Liability for Nuclear Damage (1063 U.N.T.S. 265)
1969 Vienna Convention on the Law of Treaties (VCLT) (8 ILM 679)
1971 Ramsar Convention on Wetlands of International Importance Especially as Waterfowl (996 U.N.T.S. 245)
1972 Paris Convention Concerning the Protection of the World Cultural and Natural Heritage (1037 U.N.T.S.151)
1972 London Convention on the Prevention of Marine Pollution by Dumping of Wastes and Other Matter (1046 U.N.T.S.120)
1973 Washington Convention on International Trade in Endangered Species of Wild Flora and Fauna (CITES) (983 U.N.T.S. 243)
1979 UNECE Convention on Long-Range Transboundary Air Pollution (CLRTAP) (18 ILM 1442)
1979 Bonn Convention on the Migratory Species of Wild Animals (19 ILM 15)
1982 Montego Bay Convention on the Law of the Sea (UNCLOS) (21 ILM 1261)
1985 Vienna Convention for the Protection of the Ozone Layer (26 ILM 1529)
1987 Montreal Protocol on Substances that Deplete the Ozone Layer (26 ILM 154)
1988 Sofia Protocol to CLRTAP (28 ILM 214 [1988])

1989 Basel Convention on the Control of the Transboundary Movements of Hazardous Wastes and their Disposal (28 ILM 657)

1991 Geneva Protocol to CLRTAP (31 ILM 568 [1992])

1992 Convention on Biological Diversity (31 ILM 822)

1992 UN Framework Convention on Climate Change (1771 U.N.T.S.107)

1992 International Convention on Civil Liability for Oil Pollution Damage (IMO LEG/CONF.9/15)

1992 Protocol to the Brussels Convention on the Establishment of an International Fund for Compensation of Oil Pollution Damage (BNA21: 1751)

1994 UN Convention to Combat Desertification in those Countries Experiencing Serious Drought and/or Desertification, particularly in Africa (UNCCD) (33 ILM 1328)

1994 WTO Agreement on Understanding on Rules and Procedures Governing the Settlement of Disputes (33 ILM 1125)

1995 International Agreement Relating to the Conservation of Straddling Fish Stocks and Highly Migratory Fish Stocks (34 ILM 1542)

1996 London Protocol to the 1972 London Convention on the Prevention of Marine Pollution by Dumping of Wastes and Other Matter (36 ILM 1)

1997 Kyoto Protocol to the United Nations Framework Convention on Climate Change (37 ILM 22)

1998 Rotterdam Convention on the Prior Informed Consent procedure for Certain Hazardous Chemicals and Pesticides in International Trade (38 ILM 1)

1998 UNECE Århus Convention on Access to Information, Public Participation in Decision-Making and Access to Justice in Environmental Matters (38 ILM 517)

2000 Cartagena Protocol on Biosafety (39 ILM 1027)

2001 International Treaty on Plant Genetic Resources for Food and Agriculture (www.planttreaty.org)

2001 UN Stockholm Convention on Persistent Organic Pollutants (40 ILM 532)

2001 Convention on Civil Liability for Bunker Oil Pollution Damage (40 ILM 1493)

2003 Protocol to the Brussels Convention on the Establishment of an International Fund for Compensation of Oil Pollution Damage (92FUND/A.8/4)

2015 Paris Agreement to the UN Framework Convention on Climate Change (C.N.92.2016.TREATIES-XXVII.7.d)

Other key general international instruments

1945 UN Charter of the United Nations (1 U.N.T.S XVI)
1972 UN Stockholm Conference on the Human Environment, Declaration of Principles (UN Doc.A/CONF.48/14/Rev.1)
1992 UN Rio Declaration on the Environment and Development (Doc.A/CONF.151/26/Rev.1)
1992 UNCED *Agenda 21: Programme of Action for Sustainable Development* (UNCED Report, A/CONF.151/26/Rev.1)
2001 ILC Articles on Responsibility of States for Internationally Wrongful Acts (UN Doc. A/56/10 (2001)).
2001 ILC Articles on Prevention of Transboundary Harm from Hazardous Activities (UNGA official records, 56th Session, and Suppl.No.10 (A/56/10))
2002 *Plan of Implementation* of the World Summit on Sustainable Development (A/CONF.199/20)
2002 UNEP *Guidelines on Compliance and Enforcement of Multilateral Environmental Agreements* (UNEP, SS.VII/4, 4.2.2002)
2003 UNECE *Guidelines for Strengthening Compliance and Implementation of Multilateral Environmental Agreements in the ECE Region* (ECE/CEP/107)
UNGA Resolution *The Future We Want* 66/288 of 27.7.2012 (A/RES/66/288)

European Union

EU founding treaties and other key primary EU legal sources

1957 Treaty on the European Atomic Energy Community, as amended (EAEC Treaty) (OJ 2016 C202)
1987 Single European Act (OJ 1987 L169)
1992 Treaty on European Union (TEU), as amended (OJ 2016 C202)
2007 Treaty on the Functioning of the EU (TFEU) (OJ 2016 C202)
2007 EU Charter of Fundamental Rights (OJ 2012 C83/02)
2007 Treaty of Lisbon (OJ 2007 C306)

Selected key EU legislation concerning environmental law enforcement

Regulations

Regulation 1367/2006 on the application of the provisions of the Århus Convention to Community institutions and bodies (OJ 2006 L264/13)

Directives

Directive 2003/4 on public access to environmental information (OJ 2003 L41/26)
Directive 2003/35 providing for public participation in respect of the drawing up of certain plans and programmes relating to the environment, as amended (OJ 2003 L156/17)
Directive 2004/35 on environmental liability (OJ 2004 L143/56)
Directive 2008/99 on the protection of the environment through criminal law (OJ 2008 L328/28)

Decisions

Decision 2005/370 on the conclusion, on behalf of the European Community, of the Århus Convention (OJ 2005 L124/1)
Decision 1386/2013 on a General Union Environment Action Programme to 2020 'Living well, within the limits of our planet' (OJ 2013 L354/171)

Recommendations

Recommendation 2001/331 providing for minimum criteria of environmental inspections in the member states (OJ 2001 L118/41)

Table of abbreviations

CBDR	common but differentiated responsibility
CJEU	Court of Justice of the European Union
CITES	1973 Convention on the International Trade in Endangered Species
CLRTAP	1979 Convention on Long-Range Transboundary Air Pollution
CMLRev	*Common Market Law Review*
COP	conference of the parties
ECR	European Court Reports
EEELR	*European Energy and Environmental Law Review*
EIR	Environmental Implementation Review (of the EU)
ELNI	Environmental Law Network International Review
EU	European Union
GATT	1994 General Agreement on Tariffs and Trade
GHG	greenhouse gas
IAEA	International Atomic Energy Authority
ICJ	International Court of Justice
ILC	International Law Commission
IEL	international environmental law
IMPEL	EU Network for the Implementation and Enforcement of Environmental Law
IT-PGRFA	2001 International Treaty on Plant Genetic Resources for Food and Agriculture
JEEPL	*Journal of European Environmental and Planning Law*
JEL	*Journal of Environmental Law*
ILM	International Legal Materials
ITLOS	International Tribunal for the Law of the Sea
MEA	multilateral environmental agreement
MOP	meeting of the parties
NGO	non-governmental organisation

ODS	ozone depleting substances
OECD	Organisation for Economic Co-operation and Development
OJ	Official Journal of the EU
OSPAR	1992 Convention for the Protection of the North-East Atlantic
OUP	Oxford University Press
PCA	Permanent Court of Arbitration
PIC	prior informed consent
POPs	persistent organic pollutants
RECIEL	Review of European, Comparative and International Environmental Law
REIO	regional economic integration organisation
TEU	1992 Treaty on European Union
TFEU	2007 Treaty on the Functioning of the EU
UN	United Nations
UNCLOS	1982 UN Convention on the Law of the Sea
UNECE	United Nations Economic Commission for Europe
UNEP	United Nations Environment Programme
UNGA	United Nations General Assembly
UNFCCC	1992 UN Framework Convention on Climate Change
U.N.T.S.	United Nations Treaty Series (https://treaties.un.org/)
VCLT	Vienna Convention on the Law of Treaties
WTO	World Trade Organisation

Part I

Challenges of enforcing International Environmental Law

1 Introduction

Ever since nations gathered together for the first seminal international conference on environmental protection in 1972, namely the United Nations Conference on the Human Environment in Stockholm,[1] the international community has not been found wanting in terms of generating significant numbers of multilateral environmental agreements (MEAs). The United Nations Environment Programme (UNEP) has identified over 500 agreements (regional and multilateral) now in existence relating to environmental protection issues.[2] However, delivery on MEA commitments has been far less forthcoming, with several state parties often having poor or mediocre track records on implementing international environmental treaty obligations.[3]

The system of international law is based on the premise that states, as its principal subjects, are primarily responsible for the implementation of their international duties, in so far as they do not make other arrangements by way of international agreement.[4] Whilst it is possible for states to agree with each other to endow independent entities (e.g. international bodies established under the aegis of a treaty) with powers to supervise the proper implementation of treaty obligations by contracting parties, including the power to impose coercive measures as a means of assisting in this objective, in practice very few treaty regimes concerning environmental protection have set up credible international enforcement structures and systems. Enforcement may be defined in basic general terms of being 'the process of compelling observance of a law', whilst 'sanction' may be depicted as a means to ensure the adherence to a legal requirement or set of requirements by 'attaching a penalty to transgression'.[5] Yet powers of compulsion and imposition of penalties are not elements usually embedded within with the rules and institutional structures constituting the framework of the body of international principles and agreements that collectively may be said to form the legal domain known as international environmental law (IEL). Making the writ of IEL run' by virtue of the deployment of international systems and measures designed to enhance enforcement, regrettably still remains a relatively rare as opposed to a standard occurrence.

At the same time, though, it would be fundamentally incorrect to dismiss the issue of enforcement as a matter of little relevance to the evolving legal framework of IEL. As is widely acknowledged, the establishment of means to ensure that nation states comply with their international obligations concerning environmental protection is of crucial importance to upholding IEL's credibility and effectiveness.[6] For unless states take appropriate steps to implement their IEL duties within their respective territories, the brutal reality will be that international agreements on the environment will most likely remain simply words on scrap paper rather than key tools to address regional and global environmental problems and challenges. It is a foundational tenet of international law that states must respect their international legal commitments, as reflected in the principles of *pacta sunt servanda*[7] and that a conflict with national law is not normally permissible as a defence to non-compliance with an international legal requirement.[8] Notwithstanding that these principles are well established within the corpus of international law, in practice there has been a long-standing problem of widespread non-compliance by states with MEAs,[9] not least given the fact that these principles are not self-executing within a national legal system unless stipulated or otherwise recognised to be the case by a state's constitution.

The pre-eminent status of the nation state as actors of international relations also raises significant challenges in relation to any attempt to establish international agreement over environmental problems. Whilst the environment respects no borders, international law certainly does. The principle of sovereign equality of nation states[10] which underpins the foundations of international law means that the substantive content and development of any MEA intended to address an environmental problem is dependent upon the consent of each contracting party, unless otherwise agreed. This raises the problem of how to ensure that international environmental standards avoid those favoured by the lowest common denominator. Moreover, it is also a well-established principle that states have exclusive control over activities conducted within their territorial frontiers, in so far these do not have significant adverse environmental effects elsewhere. Whilst the principle of state responsibility has emerged in international law so as to hold individual states to account for transboundary environmental damage perpetrated as a result of activities operated within their respective territories, this does not extend to damage caused to the environment located within their internal frontiers.

This short book considers in outline the contribution made by various international legal principles and treaty initiatives which have been intended to enhance the degree of statal compliance with IEL. Since the 1992 UN Conference on Environment and Development in Rio (the so-called 'Earth Summit') the international community has been increasingly mindful of the significance of the issue of IEL implementation and the need to achieve better rates of compliance with MEA commitments.[11] Particular attention will be paid to the role played by the relatively recent innovation of collective peer-review type systems instituted within a number of MEA regimes to address suspected or uncontested instances of non-compliance. These arrangements are of notable interest, precisely because they are designed to transfer, at least to some extent, control away from individual states over implementation supervision and into the hands of the collective interest of contracting parties underpinning MEA objectives.

In addition to this brief introduction, Part I spans two other short chapters. Chapters 2 and 3 place the subject of enforcement of IEL into its broader context. Chapter 2 considers the extent of problems the international community has experienced with the challenge of realising the implementation of IEL amongst contracting parties (examining the track record) as well as the general reaction to this issue as expressed at international level. Chapter 3 steps back somewhat and reflects upon the differing theoretical considerations relating to statal motivations and priorities concerning the matter of adhering to IEL requirements as well as upon the care needed when using terminology in this legal field (such as 'enforcement', 'compliance' and 'implementation'). Part II explores the range of procedural mechanisms and obligations that have been developed over time in order to address scenarios of non-compliance with international environmental obligations, taking into consideration traditional inter-statal dispute resolution principles and mechanisms as well as more recent and innovative systems of collective compliance review in various MEA systems (notably non-compliance mechanisms and the unique system of law enforcement apparatus of the European Union [EU]). Part III takes a brief look at the availability of sanctions that may be deployed at international level in respect of non-compliance with certain IEL sources before Part V concludes with some brief reflections and tentative conclusions on the prospects for international level systems of enforcement of IEL.

Notes

1 See Report of the 1972 UN Conference on the Human Environment (UN Doc. CONF.48/14/Rev.1) available for inspection at: http://www.un-documents.net/aconf48-14r1.pdf
2 See UNEP, *GEO5 Global Environment Outlook: Environment for the Future We Want* (2012) at 464 (available at: http://www.unep.org/geo/geo5.asp).
3 See e.g. Krämer (2016) at *xviii.*
4 Sands/Peel (2018) at 153.
5 *The Shorter Oxford English Dictionary* 6th ed (Oxford UP, 2007) Vol. I at 833 and Vol. II at 2661 respectively.
6 See e.g. Bodansky (2010) at 226; Boyle (1991) at 226; and Birnie/Boyle/Redgwell (2009) at 211.
7 Art.26 Vienna Convention on the Law of Treaties (VCLT) (8 ILM 679 (1969)).
8 Arts.27 and 46 VCLT.
9 See Neumayer (2012) at 4.
10 See e.g. Sands/Peel (2018) at 12 and Brownlie (1990) at 287.
11 See Section 4 'Means of Implementation' of the blueprint and action plan document for delivery of sustainable development agreed at the 1992 UNCED *Agenda 21: Programme of Action for Sustainable Development* (UNCED Report, A/CONF.151/26/Rev.1) (Vol.1) (1993) 247–284.

2 Implementation shortcomings and international reaction

As the number of international environmental agreements has increased significantly over time since the early 1970s, the international community has recognised the importance of the need to ensure and develop procedures to promote and review their full and timely implementation.[1] However, the overall track record regarding MEA implementation across the international community of states has been less than impressive. The phenomenon of 'treaty congestion' has been criticised, namely a situation characterised by a proliferation of international agreements (bilateral, regional and multilateral) concerned with particular shared environmental problems but hampered in particular by often poor delivery on treaty commitments and a lack of co-ordination between them.[2]

A number of MEA regimes have noted for several years that many contracting parties fail to honour their treaty obligations, notably with regard to the provision of national reports containing information pertinent for the purposes of assisting review on their implementation performance. A few recent examples serve to illustrate the general long-standing problem of widespread shortcomings concerning implementation. Only 13% of contracting parties submitted their annual report for 2013 on dumping permits under the aegis of the 1972 Convention on the Prevention of Marine Pollution by Dumping of Wastes and Other Matter (London Convention).[3] Only 47% of contracting parties of the 1996 London Protocol[4] to the 1972 Convention had submitted marine dumping permit reports for 2013, whilst just 25% of contracting parties had submitted their reports on implementation measures by 2015.[5] In 2013 only 50% of the contracting parties to the 1973 Washington Convention on International Trade in Endangered Species of Wild Flora and Fauna (CITES)[6] were considered by the 16th Conference of the Parties (COP) to have adopted satisfactory implementation legislation.[7] As at March 2016, significant shortcomings over data (which should have been supplied by contracting parties) affected 58% of wetland sites of international importance designated under the 1971 Convention on Wetlands of International Importance especially as Waterfowl (Ramsar Convention).[8] Between 2000 and 2014 a total of 40 non-compliance decisions were made by the Executive Body to the 1979 UNECE Convention on Long-Range Transboundary Air Pollution (CLRTAP)[9] containing 155 adverse findings against individual contracting parties in respect of reporting obligation violations. During the same period the Executive Body handed down 75 decisions confirming 78 breaches of CLRTAP provisions requiring air pollution emissions reductions by various contracting parties.[10] Some 50% and 55% of contracting parties to the 1989 UN Convention on the Control of the Transboundary Movements of Hazardous Wastes and their Disposal (Basel Convention)[11] failed to submit their national annual reports on waste data for 2011 and 2012 respectively, whilst only 0.5% and 5% of parties had reported to the Basel Secretariat in 2015 as having submitted complete reports for these two years respectively.[12] As at June 2016, only about half of contracting parties had submitted the three national implementation reports required thus far under the aegis of the 2001 UN Convention on Persistent Organic Pollutants (Stockholm Convention),[13] according to information provided by the MEA's Secretariat.[14] Only some 30% of Contracting parties to the 2000 Cartagena Protocol on Biosafety[15] (Cartagena Protocol) to the 1992 UN Convention on Biological Diversity[16] are considered to have put in place satisfactory implementation measures.[17] Whilst there have been instances where rates of compliance have been higher, this is a relatively rare occurrence and invariably only where contracting parties to the particular MEA regime have agreed to install sophisticated compliance mechanisms (such as the EU), through which a range of response measures may be ultimately deployed. These are discussed later in Part III.

For several years now concerns have been raised at international level regarding the degree of non-compliance with obligations set by international environmental accords.[18] Notably, the 2000 Malmö Ministerial Declaration[19] expressed alarm at the gap between commitments and action, recognising 'the central importance of environmental compliance, enforcement and liability'.[20] As a consequence, in 2002 the Governing Council of the United Nations Environment Programme (UNEP) adopted advisory Guidelines[21] on approaches for enhancing compliance with MEAs and strengthening the enforcement of laws implementing them. The 2002 UNEP Guidelines, subsequently endorsed with supplementary advice from UNECE,[22] are divided up into two parts. The first part contains a range of recommendations to be taken into consideration at international level with the aim of facilitating compliance with MEA obligations, including ensuring an effective negotiations process (focusing on preparation, participation and assessment of domestic capabilities) as well as taking on board considerations relevance to assisting in enhancing compliance of contracting parties. These include considering the need for textual clarity, incorporation of provisions concerning national implementation measures, capacity-building and technology transfer, performance review obligations, non-compliance mechanisms overseen by a treaty body and inter-state dispute settlement procedures as well as on fostering international co-operation. The second part focuses on providing general advice with respect to national enforcement of laws to implement MEAs, containing recommendations relating to the crafting of legislation, the administrative structuring of enforcement agencies, public education as well as measures to facilitate international co-operation and co-ordination on enforcement matters.

Notes

1 See notably Article 39 (esp. section 39.8) of 1992 UNCED *Agenda 21: Programme of Action for Sustainable Development* (UNCED Report, A/CONF.151/26/Rev.1). See also the 2002 Report of the World Summit on Sustainable Development - *Plan of Implementation of the WSSD* (Johannesburg) (A/CONF.199/20).
2 See e.g. Anton (2013) and Vidal (2012).
3 1046 U.N.T.S.120.
4 36 ILM 1 (1997).
5 See Report of 37th Consultative Meeting of the Contracting parties to the 1972 London Convention (*supra* note 3) and the 10th Meeting of Contracting parties to the 1996 London Protocol (*supra* note 4) (LC37/16, 22.10.15) and Report of 8th Meeting of the Compliance Group under the 1996 London Protocol (LC37/WP.2, 9.10.2015).
6 983 U.N.T.S. 243 (1973).
7 See COP-16 (CITES) document *CITES Interpretation and implementation of the Convention: Compliance and Enforcement* (COP-16 Doc.28, 14.3.2013).
8 996 U.N.T.S. 245. See 52nd Meeting of the Ramsar Convention Standing Committee: *Update on Status of Sites on the List of Wetlands of International Importance* (Doc. SC52–06, 13–17.6.2016).
9 18 ILM 1442 (1979).
10 From empirical research gleaned by the author from the official CLRTAP website at: http://www.unece.org/env/lrtap/executivebody/eb_decision.html
11 28 ILM 657 (1989).
12 COP-12 Report of the COP - Dec. BC-12/7: *Committee for Administering the Mechanism for Promoting Implementation and Compliance of the Basel Convention*, 4–15.5.2015.
13 40 ILM 532 (2001).

14 For information on the submission rate for the three national reports due by end 2006, end October 2010 and end August 2014 respectively provided by the POPs Convention's Secretariat at: http://chm.pops.int/Countries/Reporting/NationalReports/tabid/3668/Default.aspx
15 39 ILM 1027 (2000).
16 31 ILM 822 (1992).
17 See Report of the Cartagena Biosafety Protocol Compliance Committee, *Evaluation of the Status of Implementation of the Protocol in Meeting Its Objectives* (UNEP/CBD/BS/CC/13/3, 3.2.2016).
18 See e.g. Goetyn/Maes (2011) at 791, Sands/Peel (2018) at 144 and Hunter/Salzman/Zaelke (2011).
19 Adopted by the Global Ministerial Environment Forum – 6th Special Session of the Governing Council of the United Nations Environment Programme Fifth plenary meeting, 31 May 2000. Available at: http://www.unep.org/malmo/malmo2.pdf
20 These expressions of concern have also been voiced subsequently in other international fora. See e.g. the 2003 'Kiev Declaration' by Environment Ministers of UNECE (ECE/CEP/94/Rev1, 11.6.2003) and 2005 UNGA Resolution *World Summit Outcome* (UN Doc. A/RES/60/1, 24.20.2005) especially at para.169.
21 UNEP *Guidelines on Compliance and Enforcement of Multilateral Environmental Agreements* (UNEP, SS.VII/4, 4.2.2002).
22 UNECE *Guidelines for Strengthening Compliance and Implementation of Multilateral Environmental Agreements in the ECE Region* (ECE/CEP/107) as adopted by the Fifth UNECE Ministerial Conference Environment for Europe, Kiev, 21–23 May, 2003.

3 Reflections on terminology and theoretical perspectives concerning enforcement of International Environmental Law

Prior to examining in some detail in Part II the various sources and types of international rules concerned with enhancing or assisting with the enforcement of IEL, it is first helpful to take on board some general considerations relevant to placing this analysis in a broader legal and political context. Specifically, these concern appraising the use and definition of key terminology in this field as well as reflecting upon theoretical understandings of states' motivations to adhere to or not to their obligations under IEL.

Definitions of key terminology regarding enforcement

In any area of law, care needs to be taken with the use of terminology. Notably, accuracy and precision of terminology is a crucially important matter for the purpose of identifying the parameters of legal rights and obligations or the extent of jurisdiction. In this book, it is important to be clear about one's understanding about the role that *international* (as opposed to national) rules may have in assisting in the process of ensuring states' adherence to IEL. The use of language to describe that role is key in providing a foundational term that reflects an understanding of the actual or potential ambit or influence of that role. How then should that role be described?

The mainstream approach in international scholarship and practice might look rather sceptically at a depiction of international law and its institutions as having a role in 'enforcing' IEL. Instead, reference is commonly made to using softer terminology of international regulatory and/or institutional systems being actually or potentially involved in 'compliance' enhancement and assurance techniques. The reason for this scepticism might well in part lie in the fact that, unless otherwise agreed, international law has no jurisdiction to interfere in the internal affairs of a state by compelling the latter's public institutions or private actors to comply with an international obligation binding on that state. This understanding of the limits of the reach of international law, in terms of environmental protection, finds reflection, for instance, in Principle 2 of the UN's Rio Declaration on the Environment and Development,[1] which affirms that states have the sovereign right to exploit their own resources pursuant to their own environmental and developmental policies and the responsibility to ensure that activities within their jurisdiction or control do not cause environmental damage to areas beyond the limits of their territorial jurisdiction. As noted in the introduction, a dictionary definition of the term 'enforcement' denotes 'the process of compelling observance of a law'.[2] And yet international law, specifically IEL, does not have any general automatic command over any legal power to compel compliance, notably through the use of administrative and judicial authorities, in so far as a state does not agree to invest international bodies with such powers.

There is a general division of responsibility recognised amongst the international community of states over the respective roles of decision-makers at international and statal (national) level as far as the development of IEL is concerned, just as there is in respect of the development of international law generally. Specifically, whilst states may periodically agree with one another at international level to set common minimum rules of conduct in a particular environmental policy field (crystallised, for instance, in an international treaty) and accordingly agree that such rules should be regarded as independent sources of international law and be subject to rules of international legal interpretation, issues relating to the implementation of those international obligations within states' territories are usually regarded as matters of exclusive national legal concern, namely as matters subject to the internal decision-making of each state in accordance with its constitutional requirements. Of course, in theory it would be possible for states to agree with one another to vest international institutions (administrative and/or judicial) with powers to supervise and require adherence by contracting parties to agreed minimum standards of conduct. However, in practice it is rare for states to agree that such powers be granted to international institutions for reasons associated with a general perception amongst states that such powers would be an undue encroachment on national sovereignty. One significant exception to this general possessiveness of states over implementation matters is the European Union, whose legal order requires that Union decisions are accepted by member states as being directly enforceable at national level.[3]

The UNEP's advisory Guidelines[4] on approaches for enhancing compliance with MEAs and strengthening the enforcement of laws implementing them notably avoids reference to the term 'enforcement' in connection with the impact of international environmental rules. Tellingly, the 2002 UNEP Guidelines refer to the issue of enforcement in purely state-centric terms, defining 'enforcement' in the following terms:

> [T]he range of procedures and actions employed by a State, its competent authorities and agencies to ensure that organizations or persons, potentially failing to comply with environmental laws or regulations implementing [MEAs], can be brought or returned into compliance and/or punished through civil, administrative or criminal action.[5]

Accordingly, the term 'enforcement' is perceived here in a narrow sense to refer to the legal powers of a state to hold individuals to account in respect of a failure to observe minimum standards of conduct required by national legal rules which are intended to implement an international environmental agreement binding on that state. In contrast, the UNEP Guidelines appraise potential initiatives at international level intended to enhance statal adherence to MEA obligations in terms of a broader and softer, more diplomatically-orientated set of tools to promote compliance. Notably, non-compliance mechanisms are depicted as 'assisting parties having compliance problems and addressing individual cases of non-compliance'.[6] The UNEP Guidelines' strong emphasis on the role of national legal systems in law enforcement both underlines as well as reifies the traditional state-centric bias of international law towards the issue addressing non-compliance with MEAs.

However, I would argue that there is in fact no convincing reason to decouple the term 'enforcement' from the effects of international environmental regulation. In particular, there is no doubt an integral part of international law concerns itself with the issue of statal compliance with international obligations; international law does not defer to states totally on the matter of implementation of its rules. Notably, Article 26 of the 1969 Vienna Convention on Law of Treaties (VCLT)[7] requires contracting parties to any international treaty to perform their treaty obligations in good faith (*pacta sunt servanda*). Article 27 VCLT specifies that a party to a treaty may not invoke the provisions of its internal law as justification for its failure to perform the treaty, subject to only limited exceptions.[8] Accordingly, questions of proper implementation of IEL are not ones exclusively reserved for a national legal appraisal and international law has a clear mandate to be able to develop systems which are intended to assist in enhancing the degree to which states adhere to internationally agreed rules.

Moreover, the term 'enforcement' should not be viewed as necessarily being confined to focusing on situations concerning legal compulsion of individuals under national law as the 2002 UNEP Guidelines appear to indicate. Enforcement can also be used more broadly to encompass a role for IEL to assist in the process of ensuring that states comply with their international environmental obligations. As we have seen from the previous paragraph, international law has a clear mandate to expect that states comply with their international obligations and also develop rules that induce or otherwise facilitate statal adherence with those norms.

It is also rather misleading to depict MEA dispute resolution systems as not having a significantly influential impact on states. Admittedly, hardly any MEA regimes may be described as having the powers purporting to compel compliance or to wield sanctions on defaulting contracting parties.[9] However, a number of collective non-compliance mechanisms in MEAs now dispose of a variety of measures that are capable of having or close to having a *de facto* coercive impact, even if they are not backed up by the force of statal authority and force that underpins traditional mechanisms of law enforcement used at national level (civil, administrative and/or criminal law). These mechanisms are appraised in Part II.

Theoretical perspectives

Prior to examining the various international rules concerned with enhancing or assisting with the enforcement of IEL, it is perhaps first useful to take on board certain key theoretical arguments over why states may or may not comply with their international legal commitments, as well as related debates over policy strategy on how best to enhance statal compliance with international environmental obligations. These theories have been significant in influencing the evolution of the international legal framework. Broadly speaking, two main rival schools of thought on compliance theory in international relations have predominated in deliberation over why states may or may not comply with their international legal duties, namely a logic of consequences versus a logic of appropriateness. Likewise, two broad camps have emerged offering distinct approaches on how international law should be crafted in order to maximise compliance based on acceptance of a particular compliance theory; these being the enforcement versus managerialist approaches.[10] Whilst these rival analyses retain relevance and influence to varying degrees in the development of IEL, it is fair to say that since the early 1990s the logic of appropriateness school and related managerialist approach have gained considerable traction in legal scholarship and in international practice in terms of MEA regime building. Each will be discussed briefly in turn.

The logic of consequences school of thought, closely related to a rationalist interpretation of actor behaviour, assumes that states are motivated by weighing up the consequences of alternative course of action in light of self-interest. According to this school of thought a variety of factors may influence statal behaviour, including its relative global power, resources and internal political preferences. As far as compliance with international law is concerned, a material consideration for this theory will be the factor of deterrence. Specifically, the extent to which there are systems in place to ensure a high likelihood of detection of non-compliance coupled with sufficiently swift and costly sanctions as response measures will materially influence state decisions over whether or not to comply with an international obligation. This understanding of dynamics of statal compliance resonates strongly with deterrence theoretical models on individual personal compliance with regulation.[11]

Based closely on the theoretical underpinnings of the logic of consequences school, the enforcement approach[12] envisages that the most appropriate strategy to maximise statal compliance with international law is to ensure international accords contain deep structures of co-operation and supervision, notably including sanction mechanisms capable of tipping the cost-benefit calculation of contracting parties as to whether or not to take steps to achieve compliance.[13] Whilst the logic of consequences school has traditionally predominated in international relations discourse, in practice the enforcement approach has received a weak reception in terms of international regime-building, not least in the environmental protection sector. With a few notable exceptions,[14] relatively few MEAs contain procedures equipped for the deployment of coercive-type sanctions against non-compliant contracting parties. Whilst, for instance, a range of MEAs do contain non-compliance mechanisms which envisage the possibility of imposing a limited range of response measures on defaulting contracting parties (as discussed in Part IV below), the most coercive tool options (such as suspension of treaty rights/privileges or the imposition of financial penalties) are only infrequently deployed in international practice as a means of last resort.

In contrast, the logic of appropriateness school of thought views the dynamics and motivations of statal compliance with international law in a radically different way. Its principal assumption is that states operate essentially as good faith actors generally wishing to comply with their international obligations and view their fulfilment as socially legitimate. This theory considers that a state is motivated also by a consideration that the greater degree to which it complies with freely assumed obligations, the more positive an image will be given to other states regarding its international standing. At the same time, this theoretical perspective acknowledges that sometimes states may not always be able to fulfil their international duties, but accounts for this largely as a result of capacity issues rather than any deliberate strategy on the part of a state to be deviant.

In the 1990s, notably through the work of Chayes and Chayes,[15] a managerial model emerged from this theoretical foundation for the purposes of developing a strategic response to the challenge of enhancing the state of implementation with international rules of law, including IEL. Contrary to the enforcement approach, a managerialist perspective envisions IEL regimes to be regarded as instruments to manage an environmental protection field over time rather than be underpinned by sets of prohibitory rules. The overall approach advocated is to install a system so as to keep non-compliance to acceptable levels primarily through a continual process of transparent discourse and exchange amongst contracting parties (typically through education, advice and/or assistance). Managerialism's general assumption is that states intend to comply with their environmental treaty obligations and that instances of non-compliance will be largely due to capacity issues or inadvertence (e.g. lack of national legislative, administrative and/or financial resources) rather than any deliberate intent to breach an international provision. Accordingly, the managerialist approach favours prioritising facilitative responses in order to address issues of non-compliance with MEAs, whilst not discounting the possibility of using more coercive response measures as a last resort in the face of persistent offending. It has received considerable endorsement within international legal scholarship[16] and has exerted a significant degree of influence on the way in which several MEA regimes have developed systems to enhance statal compliance.

Both the enforcement and managerial approaches as well as theories underpinning them are widely accepted as bringing useful insights to bear on the way in which prescriptive MEA regimes should be crafted.[17] Whilst starting from contrasting assumptions and promoting different techniques, the two approaches on strategy are not necessarily mutually incompatible.[18] For instance, the managerial camp would not completely rule out the use of sanctions as a last resort tool, whilst a broad understanding of the meaning and tiering of non-compliance response measures would not necessarily be ruled out under an enforcement approach.

Notes

1 UN Doc. A/CONF.151/26/Rev.1
2 *The Shorter Oxford English Dictionary* 6th ed (Oxford UP, 2007) Vol. I at 833.
3 See, for instance, Articles 280 and 299 of the 2007 Treaty on the Functioning of the EU (TFEU) which require judgments of the EU Court of Justice or other EU acts imposing pecuniary obligations on individuals to be enforceable via the national civil procedural rules of the EU member states.
4 UNEP *Guidelines on Compliance and Enforcement of Multilateral Environmental Agreements* (UNEP, SS.VII/4, 4.2.2002).
5 Para. 38(d), ibid.
6 Ibid.
7 8 ILM 679 (1969).
8 See Article 46 VCLT.
9 The European Union may be regarded as an exception in this regard (see Chapter 6 of Part III, this text).
10 For some overviews and reflections on compliance theory see e.g. Mitchell (2007) at 893, Zaelke/Higdon (2006), Brunnée J (2005) at 1 and Bodansky (2010) at 226.
11 See notably Becker (1968).
12 See for a view in favour of this approach: see e.g. Downs/Rocke/Barsoom (1996) at 379.
13 See Mitchell (2007) at 912.
14 In particular, CITES and the European Union (see Part III).
15 Chayes/Chayes (1993) at 175–205.
16 See e.g. Brown Weiss/Jacobson (2000), Bodansky (2010) Chapters 10–11, O'Connell (1995) and Goteyn/Maes (2011) at 800.
17 See e.g. Zaelke/Higdon (2006) at 383 and Goteyn /Maes (2011) at 801.
18 See e.g. Bodansky (2010) at 238.

Part II

The international legal framework relating to the enforcement of International Environmental Law

4 Traditional bilateral dispute resolution principles and mechanisms

That the record of implementation of MEAs has been and remains far from satisfactory should be of little surprise given the limits of international law's reach in relation to enforcement matters. As mentioned in the introduction, power to regulate over implementation matters remains in principle a national competence in the absence of states agreeing to vest supervisory authority in an independent entity at international level. Whilst over many years international law has recognised and developed ways and means for states to assert their territorial integrity or international treaty rights against one another, it has not been structured so as to be readily capable of supervising adherence to international environmental obligations independently of statal interference or influence.

Historically, enforcement of international obligations at international level has been considered essentially in bilateral terms, namely as disputes to be settled between states. Rules of international law have been developed over the course of several years through custom and treaties to establish and refine the procedural and substantive ground rules to assist in the peaceable resolution of inter-statal disputes. However, these classical ground rules are manifestly ill-suited to safeguard collective environmental protection goals and requirements enshrined in MEAs, especially as they foresee states as principal gatekeepers over decisions as to whether international legal action should be taken to respond to a violation of international legal obligations. At the same time, it is states who are in control over determining to what extent MEAs may contain systems designed to apply some degree of coercive influence on contracting parties in the event of the latter failing to honour their legal duties to protect the environment. These, as will be explored later in Part II, may include the establishment of collective or independent compliance review mechanisms. In practice, and unsurprisingly, states have shown little motivation to pursue claims against one another over alleged breaches of international environmental obligations unless their particular individual interests are threatened or damaged in some way.

Given the state-centric orientation of international law, Bodansky's comment that the area of law enforcement has 'never been a strong suit' of IEL is particularly apt.[1] Nevertheless, IEL does have some cards to play here. The following sub-sections analyse the contribution made by existing sources of international law with respect to assisting in the enforcement of international environmental obligations.

Classically, the ground rules addressing questions of enforcement of sources of internationally binding environmental commitments have been based upon general tenets of international law relating to state responsibility for the purpose of resolving of inter-statal disputes. These are reflective of an international legal system designed primarily for safeguarding the interests of states and promoting peaceable co-existence between them; the environment is not an interest inherently protected under international law. The extent to which general international rules of law serve to offer legal protection against environmental degradation is essentially dependent upon whether such protection is covered by international obligations owed by states to one other.

The principle of state responsibility

It is a fundamental and well-established tenet of international law that states may be held to account by other states in respect of a violation of an international obligation owed to them. The recognition of the right of states to raise claims concerning the international legal responsibility of other states is restated in Article 42 of the 2001 draft Articles on Responsibility of States for Internationally Wrongful Acts[2] of the International Law Commission (ILC), the international body established by the UN General Assembly (UNGA)[3] to promote the progressive development of international law and its codification. Article 42 states:

> A State is entitled as an injured State to invoke the responsibility of another State if the obligation breached is owed to:
> (a) that State individually; or
> (b) a group of States including that State, or the international community as a whole, and the breach of obligation
> (i) specially affects that State: or

(ii) is of such a character as radically to change the position of all other States to which the obligation is owed with respect to the further performance of that obligation.

State responsibility under international law may be engaged either by a breach of a norm of customary international law[4] or treaty. As far as the former international legal source is concerned, the most relevant customary international legal norm for environmental purposes is the general duty incumbent on states to ensure that activities within their jurisdiction or control do not cause transboundary harm. The so-called 'no harm' norm, having been originally expressed in written form in Principle 21 of the 1972 UN Stockholm Declaration,[5] has been subsequently consolidated in Principle 2 of the 1992 UN Rio Declaration:[6]

> States have, in accordance with the Charter of the United Nations and the principles of international law, the sovereign right to exploit their own resources pursuant to their own environmental and developmental policies, and the responsibility to ensure that activities within their jurisdiction or control do not cause damage to the environment of other States or of areas beyond the limits of national jurisdiction.

From an international judicial perspective, the 'no harm' principle was formally recognised as a customary international norm by the International Court of Justice (ICJ) in the *Use of Nuclear Weapons* case,[7] and its environmental protection dimension may be traced to the famous arbitral decision in the US-Canadian air pollution dispute in *Trail Smelter.* [8]

The ILC also adopted in 2001 draft Articles on Prevention of Transboundary Harm from Hazardous Activities[9] which assert a complementary preventative dimension to state responsibility with respect to hazardous activities. The draft Articles include reference to statal duties to take all appropriate measures to prevent significant transboundary harm or at any event minimise the risk thereof, to undertake a transboundary impact assessment as well to notify and consult with states subject to a risk of significant transboundary harm.[10] International jurisprudence from the ICJ and other international judicial bodies has also confirmed that state responsibility is underpinned by principles of prevention[11] and good faith co-operation.[12]

International rules on the rights of states to take action in respect of breach of treaty obligations are also well-established in international law, notably reflected in the 1969 Vienna Convention on Law of

Treaties (VCLT).[13] The ILC's 2001 draft Articles on State Responsibility[14] consolidate the corpus of rules concerning remedial action available to injured states *vis-a-vis* the responsible state.

It is evident in practice that, notwithstanding their longstanding nature and evolution, rules on state responsibility have only been engaged relatively rarely by states in the context of transboundary environmental disputes. It is apparent that when they have been pursued formally, state responsibility claims over environmental protection related issues have been made typically in the context of bilateral disputes, namely where a state claimant may consider that another (usually neighbouring) state has contravened international law and as a result injured or threatened their sovereign legal interests in some way.[15] Claims are rarely, if ever, made for the purpose of upholding collective environmental protection interests.[16] Various factors, technical and political, serve to explain why states have sought to resolve environmental disputes through international litigation based on state responsibility relatively infrequently.

From a technical legal perspective, it is apparent that the current international legal framework is undermined by a number of serious shortcomings. These include the lack of legal certainty concerning the scope of the 'no harm' principle, in particular with respect to understanding sufficiently precisely when a state has failed to adhere to the underlying requirement of due diligence and when the threshold of significance in relation to harm has been exceeded. Other problems concern the limitations of state responsibility as a means of addressing transboundary environmental degradation. Notably, a claimant state's case will collapse if it is unable to provide evidence of a particular state as being the principal or contributory cause of significant harm. This will be challenging in the context of many types of global environmental problems (e.g. air and marine pollution, climate change, ozone layer depletion). Moreover, the invocation of state responsibility is entirely at the behest of the injured state concerned, which is likely to focus on a broader range of concerns and factors than purely environmental protection when weighing up whether to launch a formal claim, such as diplomatic and economic interests.

The state-centric[17] nature of state responsibility is also underpinned in terms of its limits regarding legal standing (*locus standi*) requirements for claimant states. Whilst the 'no harm' norm is clearly recognised to apply in theory also with respect to damage perpetrated in areas outside statal territorial control, it is by no means clear under what circumstances a state will have legal standing to bring a claim against another in respect of damage perpetrated by the latter in areas located outside any national jurisdiction. For instance, in the *Fur Seals* case[18] the arbitral tribunal rejected a United States claim of entitlement to protect fur seals extra-territorially on the high seas against the UK. The ICJ has signalled in the *Barcelona Traction* case[19] that an *actio popularis* claim, namely one brought by one or more states in the general public interest as opposed to a claim in response to a specific injury sustained by the claimant, might be possible where an obligation is owed to all states (*erga omnes*); however, this point has yet to be definitively confirmed and clarified by the Court.[20] According to the ILC, such a claim would be admissible.[21] The ILC also asserts it would be technically possible for a contracting party to a MEA to have standing to invoke state responsibility of another contracting party in connection with the breach by the latter of a treaty obligation 'owed to a group of States including that State, and it is established for the protection of a collective interest of the group'.[22] However, experience has shown it is very unlikely that a state will be prepared to bring an international claim purely on behalf of the environment in the absence of some clearly defined domestic interest.

Additional procedural hurdles and problems attend the prosecution of state responsibility claims in environmental disputes. In the absence of agreement between disputants, no international court has jurisdiction to hear a claim. The ICJ's jurisdiction is not mandatory under general rules of international law. Moreover, proceedings before the ICJ are relatively cumbersome, costly and protracted affairs. Of course, as with any litigation claimants must weigh up the risks of not succeeding on the merits; sometimes a case may result in the ICJ instructing disputant states to resume negotiations rather than declaring a definitive outcome.[23]

Even if a state claimant is able to invoke state responsibility successfully, the remedies available to it may not necessarily be suitable to address the underlying causes giving rise to actual or threatened environmental damage. International rules cater for the needs of states sustaining injury as a consequence of internationally wrongful acts, in being entitled to seek reparation[24]or take countermeasures.[25] However, they are far less suitable to address situations in which collective environmental interests have been wronged. Whilst Article 60 VCLT entitles a contracting party to an international treaty to terminate or suspend its operation in whole or in part in the event of material breach by another contracting party, such action would not lend itself to assisting in correcting the breach and improving the situation prospectively from an environmental perspective.[26] Moreover, states invoking responsibility against others in the collective interest for non-material breaches of a treaty appear only entitled to claim cessation of the wrongful act and assurances of non-repetition, unless they agree otherwise as a group. For the general default position is that counter-measures and reparation may only be taken and claimed by or on behalf of injured states.[27]

Over and above technical considerations, there are more profound reasons why state responsibility claims are often ill-suited to addressing transboundary environmental disputes. Retrospective and static in nature, they are unable to take on board and/or regulate ongoing environmental problems in a more suitably preventative, as opposed to reactionary, manner.[28] The complexity and dynamism of transboundary and global environmental challenges sought to be addressed by many contemporary MEAs require collective, comprehensive and proactive management, as opposed to reactive litigation focusing on the behaviour of a single state.[29] The collective interest underpinning many global MEA obligations are not suited to be addressed in terms of the traditional binary inter-statal dispute setting foreseen by the legal framework of state responsibility. The latter incorrectly assumes states to be the primary actors in seeking compliance with international environmental legal requirements.[30] It is also unable to be sufficiently nuanced so as to take on board the relevance of any lack of capacity on the part of a defendant state that may be directly connected with the breach of international law.[31] Likewise, state responsibility is blind to the principle of common but differentiated responsibility (CBDR) which has become a key integral component of contemporary IEL and policy,[32] notwithstanding that non-compliance with international environmental obligations is frequently attributable to a lack of resources on the part of several countries with developing economies. Moreover, recourse to international litigation is inherently adversarial and confrontational. It is clear that states will seek to avoid taking legal action against one another where at all possible, not least because of potential adverse costs that may arise relationally between them (e.g. diplomatically and/or economically).

Interstatal dispute settlement procedures in MEAs

Despite the limitations of the classical approach of international law in envisaging states as having a leading law enforcement role in upholding international environmental obligations, it is evident that states maintain a keen interest in ensuring that inter-state dispute settlement procedures are woven into the legal fabric of several MEAs. Dispute settlement clauses constitute a conscious effort on the part of contacting parties to implement the general legal duty on states enshrined in Article 33(1) of the UN Charter[33] to seek pacific settlement of their inter-statal disputes which stipulates that:

> The parties to any dispute, the continuance of which is likely to endanger the maintenance of international peace and security, shall, first of all, seek a solution by negotiation, enquiry, mediation, conciliation, arbitration, judicial settlement, resort to regional agencies or arrangements, or other peaceful means of their own choice.

Whilst the earlier generations of international environmental accord tended not to make any specific provision for dispute settlement,[34] the inclusion of dispute settlement procedures in MEAs has steadily increased over time.[35] It is unsurprising that procedures have been included in MEA regimes which involve a clear bilateralist dimension to them, namely where non-compliance with an obligation by one contracting party could cause direct injury to or otherwise adversely affect the particular interests of another contracting party.[36] Yet it is notable that dispute settlement procedures have also become a common feature in MEAs intended to address regional or global environmental problems, in respect of which environmental damage may be diffuse and attributed to a large number of sources.[37] This development underlines that states are keen to maintain a legal pathway for themselves to be able take unilateral action in order to uphold their treaty rights against other contracting parties, where necessary. That states are keen to retain control over the dispute resolution process at international level is further underpinned by the fact that there are very few MEAs that endow international institutions with powers to undertake formal legal proceedings against defaulting contracting parties.[38]

Whilst dispute settlement procedural provisions do vary amongst MEAs, several follow a basic standard process, with the most recent generation of agreements usually stipulating more sophisticated arrangements. The dispute settlement process foreseen in such a treaty may be typically divided into two broadly distinct phases, namely diplomatic and then adjudicatory. As a first step, contracting parties are invariably required as a first step to undertake efforts to settle quarrels diplomatically through bilateral negotiation and/or consultation. Should negotiations or consultations fail, several MEAs make reference to more formal procedures becoming available, involving the intervention or assistance from a third party in the form of mediation or conciliation. Some MEAs make it a legal requirement for contracting parties to seek resolution through conciliation as a default position, in which a third person investigates details and makes non-binding proposals.[39] Several MEAs refer to the possibility of adjudicatory means of settlement via binding arbitration or recourse to an international court such as the ICJ. However, the vast majority of MEAs make recourse to arbitration or judicial settlement dependent upon the mutual consent of the disputing parties, with a few notable exceptions.[40] Consequently, the operative success of the vast majority of dispute settlement procedures in MEAs relies essentially upon the goodwill and co-operation of disputing parties and is far more susceptible to being ultimately a negotiating as opposed to a rule of law process.

Accordingly, it might be questioned whether it would be accurate to depict voluntary dispute settlement procedures deployed in the vast majority of MEAs as genuine enforcement tools.[41] It appears evident that states have remained reluctant to develop compulsory dispute resolution procedures in most MEAs, the outcomes of which may be perceived as unpredictable and potentially expensive.[42] Another problem that may arise is the lack of co-ordination between dispute settlement procedures in the event that two or MEA regimes are relevant to a particular environmental dispute, as was evidenced for instance in the litigation between Ireland and the UK over the mixed oxide nuclear plant at Sellafield which involved proceedings in three separate international judicial fora.[43]

Whilst recourse to dispute settlement procedures have been important in relation to addressing bilateral environmental disputes, especially with regard to issues over fisheries management,[44] shared watercourses[45] and air pollution cases where the source of pollution may be traceable to a particular state,[46] overall they are rarely used in practice to uphold international environmental obligations.[47] Fundamentally, dispute settlement procedures share the same core problems as the international legal framework regarding state responsibility. Namely, they are ill-suited to for the purpose of upholding MEA obligations intended to address regional or global environmental problems and challenges. In many cases individual contracting parties lack sufficient incentive to take action against other parties for the purpose of upholding MEA rules in the collective interest, where environmental damage is diffuse and displaced and where taking action may come with an actual or potential significant (diplomatic and/or financial cost).[48]

Notes

1 Bodansky (2010) at 227.
2 UN Doc.A/56/10 (2001).
3 UNGA Res. 174(III) (1947).
4 Customary international law is a source of international law established by state practice and *opinio juris* (evidence of a belief that the practice is binding), as acknowledged in Article 38(1)(b) of the Statute of the ICJ, subject to a state having persistently objected to such a rule. For further discussion see e.g. Sands/Peel (2018) 119–125 and Birnie/Boyle/Redgwell (2009) 22–25.
5 1972 UN Conference on the Human Environment, Declaration of Principles (UN Doc.A/CONF.48/14/Rev.1).
6 1992 Rio Declaration on Environment and Development (UN Doc.A/CONF.151/26/Rev.1).
7 *Advisory Opinion of the ICJ on Legality of the Threat or Use of Nuclear Weapons* (1996) ICJ Reports 226.
8 See *Trail Smelter Arbitration (US v Canada)* (1941) RIAA 1907 in which the arbitral tribunal confirmed that under international law 'no state has the right to use or permit the use of territory in such a manner as to cause injury by fumes in or to the territory of another of the properties or persons therein, when the case is of serious consequence and the injury is established by clear and convincing evidence.'
9 Official Records of UNGA, 56th Session, and Suppl.No.10 (A/56/10).
10 See Arts. 3, 7 and 8 of the International Law Commission's 2001 *Articles on Prevention of Transboundary Harm from Hazardous Activities* (Official Records of UNGA, 56th Session, and Suppl.No.10 (A/56/10)).
11 See e.g. *Pulp Mills on the River Uruguay (Argentina v Uruguay)* (2010) ICJ Reports 18 at para. 101; *Iron Rhine Arbitration* PCA (Case 2003–02) (24.5.2005) at paras. 59 and 222.
12 See e.g. *Lac Lanoux Arbitration (Spain v France)* (1957) 24 ILR 101; *The MOX Plant Case (Provisional Measures) (Ireland v UK)* ITLOS (2002) 41 ILM 405 at para. 83.
13 8 ILM 679 (1969).
14 *Report of the ILC to the UN General Assembly* (UN Doc. A/56/10 (2001)).
15 Most of the leading sources of international jurisprudence on international environmental law have resulted from bilateral disputes between states: e.g. *Trail Smelter* (*supra* note 8), *Lac Lanoux* (*supra* note 12), *Gabcikovo-Nagymaros (Hungary v Slovakia)* (1997) ICJ Reports 7, *Pulp Mills* (*supra* note 11), *MOX Plant Case* (*supra* note 12), *Iron Rhine Arbitration* (*supra* note 11).
16 Even the claims brought by Australia and New Zealand against France in the 1970s in relation to nuclear weapons testing in the south Pacific region, whilst technically founded on the basis of a claim to uphold obligations owed *erga omnes*, was clearly driven in substantial part by concerns over nuclear fall-out within the claimant states' territories: see *Australia v France (Interim Protection)* (1973) ICJ Reports 99; (Judgment) (1974) ICJ Reports 253 and *New Zealand v France (Interim Protection)* (1973) ICJ Reports 135; (Judgment) (1974) ICJ Reports 457. The proceedings were withdrawn before the ICJ had an opportunity to adjudicate on the merits.

17 See Boyle (1991) at 229.
18 *Behring Sea Fur Seals Fisheries Arbitration (UK v US)* [1898] 1 *Moore's International Arbitration Awards* 755.
19 (1970) ICJ Reports 1.
20 Peel (2001) at 86.
21 See Art.48(1)(b) of the International Law Commission's (ILC) 2001 draft *Articles on Responsibility of States for Internationally Wrongful Acts.* However, this provision's material scope is not clear.
22 Art.48(1)(a), ibid.
23 See e.g. *Gabcikovo-Nagymaros (Hungary v Slovakia)* (*supra* note 15).
24 In the form of restitution, compensation and/or satisfaction as set out in Arts. 34–39 draft ILC Articles (*supra* n21).
25 Arts.49–53, ibid.
26 Klabbers (2007) at 102.
27 See Arts 48(2) and 54 of ILC's draft *Articles on State Responsibility* (*supra* note 21). See Peel (2001) at 87.
28 Cardesa-Salzmann (2011) at 112.
29 Ibid.
30 Boyle (1991) at 229.
31 See Brunnée (2005) at 7.
32 Principle 7 of the 1992 Rio Declaration (UN Doc.A/CONF.48/14/Rev.1).
33 UN Charter (1 U.N.T.S. xvi).
34 Examples include the 1972 Paris Convention Concerning the Protection of the World Cultural and Natural Heritage (1037 U.N.T.S.151), 1946 International Convention for the Regulation of Whaling (161 U.N.T.S.72) and the 1971 Ramsar Convention on Wetlands of International Importance especially as Waterfowl Habitat (996 U.N.T.S. 245). CITES (983 U.N.T.S. 243) is a notable exception.
35 Romano (2007) at 1040 notes that whereas 33% of MEAs included dispute settlement clauses in 1980 this figure had increased to over 50% by 2000.
36 Examples of these types of MEAs include: the 1989 Basel Convention (UN Convention on the Control of Transboundary Movements of Hazardous Waste and their Disposal) (28 ILM 657 (1989)), 1998 Rotterdam Convention on the Prior Informed Consent Procedure for Certain Hazardous Chemicals and Pesticides in International Trade (PIC Convention) (38 ILM 1 (1999)) and the 2000 Biosafety Protocol to the 1992 Convention on Biological Diversity (39 ILM 1027 (2000)).
37 For example, MEAs concerning climate change (e.g. 1992 UN Framework Convention on Climate Change (1771 U.N.T.S.107)) or ozone depletion (e.g. 1985 Vienna Convention for the Protection of the Ozone Layer (26 ILM 1529 (1985))).
38 The notable exceptions include the International Seabed Authority, which has power to sue states over illegal exploitation of the deep seabed and damage to the marine environment from seabed activities (Art.187 UN Convention on the Law of the Sea (UNCLOS) (21 ILM 1261 (1982))) and the European Commission of the European Union, which has power to sue member states over non-compliance with EU environmental law (Arts.258 and 260 TFEU). See discussion of EU later in Part II. A recommendation in 1987 by a legal expert group to the World Commission on the Environment that international institutions be established for the purposes of

assisting law enforcement akin to that applicable in the international human rights field (UN High Commissioner and Commission for the Environment) have so far not been taken up by the international community; see e.g. Rinceneau (2000) at 167.

39 For example: Art. 27 of the 1992 Convention on Biological Diversity (31 ILM 822 (1992)); Art.32 of the 2000 Biosafety Protocol (*supra* note 36); Art.28 of the 1994 UN Convention to Combat Desertification in those Countries Experiencing Serious Drought and/or Desertification, particularly in Africa (33 ILM 1328 (1994)); Art.20 of the 1998 Rotterdam Convention (*supra* note 36); Art.18 of the 2001 Stockholm Convention (UN Convention on Persistent Organic Pollutants (40 ILM 532 (2001))); Art.11 of the 1985 Vienna Convention (*supra* note 37); Art.14 of the 1987 Montreal Protocol on Substances that Deplete the Ozone Layer (26 ILM 154 (1987)); and Art.14 of the 1992 UNFCCC (*supra* note 37).

40 The principal exceptions include several MEAs concerning the marine sector, see notably: Arts.286–287 of the 1982 UN Convention on Law of the Sea (UNCLOS) (21 ILM 1261 (1982)); Art. 27 of the 1995 Agreement Relating to the Conservation of Straddling Fish Stocks and Highly Migratory Fish Stocks (34 ILM 1542 (1995)); Art.16 of the 1996 London Protocol to the 1972 Convention on the Prevention of Marine Pollution by Dumping of Wastes and Other Matter ((1997) 36 ILM 1). See also the Annex to the 1994 WTO Agreement on Understanding on Rules and Procedures Governing the Settlement of Disputes (33 ILM 1125 (1994)). In addition, the European Union falls within this exceptional category by reason of its conferral of mandatory jurisdiction to the Court of Justice of the EU (Art.344 TFEU) – see for more details in Chapter 6.

41 See Bodansky (2010) at 246.

42 UNEP *Compliance Mechanisms Under Selected Multilateral Environmental Agreements* (2007) at 119.

43 Namely before the International Tribunal on Law of the Sea (*The MOX Plant Case (Provisional Measures) (Ireland v UK)* ITLOS No.10 (2001), an Arbitration Tribunal established under the aegis of the 1992 OSPAR Convention (*MOX Plant Arbitration (Jurisdiction and Provisional Measures)* PCA (2008) (Case 2002–01) and the Court of Justice of the EU (Case C-459/03 *Commission v Ireland* [2006] ECR I-4635). See e.g. Bell/McGillivray/Pedersen (2017) at 158 and Romano (2007) at 1044.

44 For example, *Fisheries Jurisdiction (UK v Norway)* (1974) ICJ Reports 116, *Estai Case (Canada v Spain)* (1998) ICJ Reports 432, *Southern Blue Fin Tuna (Australia and New Zealand v Japan)* (2000) 39 ILM 1359.

45 See e.g. *Lac Lanoux* (*supra* note 12), *Gabcikovo* (*supra* note 15) and *Pulp Mills* (*supra* note 11) cases.

46 See e.g. *Trail Smelter* case (*supra* note 8) and *Aerial Herbicide Spraying (Ecuador v Columbia)* (2008–13) (settled and withdrawn before ICJ adjudicated on merits: (2013) ICJ Reports 278).

47 Romano (2007) at 1041 and Bodansky (2010) at 246.

48 Bodansky (2010) at 247.

5 The role of collective compliance mechanisms in International Environmental Law

As increasing numbers of MEAs became adopted in the wake of the seminal 1972 UN Stockholm Conference on the Human Environment in order to address a wide range of global environmental problems, the international community became faced with the challenge as how to ensure that such treaty regimes were equipped effectively to address implementation shortcomings. It was not long before the traditional rules of state responsibility and dispute settlement procedural mechanisms became exposed as being clearly inadequate in themselves to provide effective supervision of MEA obligations. As states began to strike agreements that moved beyond purely bilateral issues to seek to address broader environmental problems and challenges of a multilateral nature and scope, in respect of which states could not be readily identified in terms of individual blame or victimhood, it became evident that the traditional inter-state dispute resolution framework anchored in the general tenets of international law and the standard classical format of dispute settlement procedures for international treaties (envisaging disputes arising between particular contracting parties) needed to be supplemented by more effective collective supervisory mechanisms capable of serving the common as opposed to purely internal statal interests.[1]

Gradually, a new approach to addressing non-compliance with MEA obligations began to take root. Specifically, this took the form of contracting parties agreeing to establish, and in several instances then subsequently deepen, certain collective compliance mechanisms enshrined within the legal fabric of MEAs to serve as a complement to the traditional forms of dispute resolution.

Overview of non-compliance procedures in MEAs

Collective compliance mechanisms within the context of international environmental relations may be understood broadly to encompass a body of provisions and procedures organised under the auspices of a MEA which are intended to facilitate and encourage contracting parties to implement their treaty obligations. Such mechanisms may often dispose of a relatively wide range of legal tools, including notably provisions requiring information gathering and monitoring through to collective non-compliance procedures, which may be invoked against defaulting party to examine, appraise and ultimately resolve an instance of an alleged breach of the MEA in question. Irrespective of whether a MEA has established a non-compliance procedure for addressing breaches, the basis for any credible collective compliance system is the existence of obligations requiring contracting parties to provide information periodically on steps taken to implement the MEA's requirements into national law and administrative practice, as well as provision for periodic review by the MEA membership (e.g. at the conference of the parties [COP]) of implementation performance.

Several if not most MEAs provide for some kind of periodic implementation review process, typically requiring contracting parties to exchange and impart information on certain matters (e.g. reporting on implementation measures and monitoring of activities pertinent to the MEA), as part of their primary operational obligations.[2] Usually MEAs are reliant on contracting parties to self-report, with any independent monitoring or verification carried out by treaty bodies or other third parties (e.g. accredited NGOs) in contracting party territories being contingent on the consent of the party concerned. MEAs vary greatly in terms of range and intensity of compliance mechanisms they employ. For instance, some of the earliest generation[3] as well as framework[4] international environmental agreements do not foresee or otherwise provide for the establishment of non-compliance procedures and rely effectively on reporting and collective monitoring systems to review the implementation performance of contracting parties.

Those MEAs which do employ non-compliance procedures[5] differ widely in terms of the scope for review as well as response measures available to address instances of non-compliance. Such procedures usually emphasise a distinctly non-adversarial and non-confrontational approach, underpinned by the fact that the entity (committee) charged with overseeing the process for examining and appraising instances of alleged non-compliance is usually (although not always) composed of contracting party representatives. This exudes the character of an intergovernmentalist peer-review as opposed to independent supranational quasi-judicial process.

Whilst reporting and monitoring requirements are important for the purpose of encouraging and inducing contracting parties to ensure fulfilment of MEA requirements as well as identifying gaps in implementation, in themselves they provide little in the way of external coercive pressure and are ultimately reliant on parties to take them seriously. The presence of a non-compliance procedure within a MEA does, however, constitute a more direct and meaningful system for the purposes of assisting with the enforcement of MEA obligations. Such a procedure is specifically intended to be able to address shortcomings in relation to implementation and is effectively subject to external, independent oversight and control. Accordingly, the remainder of this chapter will focus specifically on the role of non-compliance procedures as part of MEA initiatives for enhancing contracting party adherence to international environmental treaty obligations.

Non-compliance procedures are usually overseen by a dedicated MEA committee (typically an implementation or compliance committee composed of contracting party representatives) and are intended to verify instances of suspected non-compliance by a contracting party and appraise whether certain collective response measures should be taken as a means of inducing a restoration of compliance. Usually, decisions over response measures are a matter for the COP, with the relevant non-compliance committee having only powers of recommendation.

MEAs vary greatly in terms of the type of collective non-compliance mechanisms they use with a view to enhance party compliance. However, such mechanisms share common fundamental characteristics which distinguish them from the formal, legalistic and adjudicative-type dispute resolution procedures and principles traditionally provided as international ground rules for states wishing to raise claims relating to non-fulfilment of international legal obligations. Essentially, all MEA non-compliance mechanisms are intended to be essentially informal, facilitative, non-adversarial and consensual in nature. Their overall approach is collegiate rather than adversarial in nature, intended to encourage and assist contracting parties in maintaining or, where shown to be in breach, returning over a reasonable period of time to a state of compliance.

The 2002 UNEP Guidelines on Compliance and Enforcement with MEAs,[6] which lays down some basic benchmarks on the use of collective compliance mechanisms, depicts their role in the following broad and flexible terms:

> Non-compliance mechanisms could be used by the contracting parties to provide a vehicle to identify possible situations of non-compliance at an early stage and the causes of non-compliance,

> and to formulate appropriate responses including, addressing and/or correcting the state of non-compliance without delay. These responses can be adjusted to meet varying requirements of cases of non-compliance, and may include both facilitative and stronger measures as appropriate and consistent with applicable international law.[7]

What has been of particular interest and significance is the innovative role that non-compliance mechanisms have come to play in practice in several MEA regimes and this chapter will proceed to consider briefly three examples in MEAs before commenting more generally on their development and effectiveness.

1987 Montreal Protocol Implementation Committee

An important milestone in the development of non-compliance mechanisms in IEL came with the establishment for the first time in 1990 of a new collective dispute resolution procedure supervised and managed by a special committee structure under the aegis of Article 8 of the 1987 Montreal Protocol on Substances that Deplete the Ozone Layer,[8] adopted under the aegis of the 1985 Vienna Convention on Protection of the Ozone Layer.[9] Whilst it is true that prior to this, CITES[10] had already initiated a process for implementation supervision via standing committee recommendations for trade suspensions in response to illicit international trade in endangered species, its approach until 2000 was essentially *ad hoc* in nature and partial in material scope.[11]

The Montreal Protocol was adopted in order to introduce specific controls on contracting parties to the 1985 Vienna Convention regarding the management of certain ozone depleting substances (ODS), referred to as controlled substances. The Protocol imposes a range of restrictions on the production, consumption and trade in controlled substances, crafted with a view to their eventual phasing out over set periods. Originally targeting 10 chemicals, the Protocol has been gradually extended to cover over 90 ODS. Most recently, the Protocol has introduced amendments to increase controls on certain ODS or replacement substances (HFCs) which have a high global-warming potential.[12]

The Montreal Protocol's Implementation Committee, made permanent in 1992[13] and whose procedures were amended in 1998,[14] lies at the heart of the procedure in constituting the treaty body which assesses claims made to it of non-compliance and making recommendations as to any follow up measures to be taken to the meeting of the parties (MOP). The Implementation Committee is composed of ten members elected by the MOP every two years, based on equitable geographical distribution, and meets at least twice a year. The MEA's non-compliance procedure may be commenced or 'triggered' in three ways, namely either: (1) by a contracting party which considers it might be (liable to be) in breach (self-trigger); (2) by other contracting parties or (3) by the MEA's secretariat becoming aware of non-compliance. Once triggered, the Implementation Committee then assesses the matter and makes appropriate recommendations to the MOP. The MOP has agreed to an indicative list of measures that be taken by it, notably assistance (including technical and financial assistance, training and information and technology transfer), cautions or suspension of specific rights and privileges under the Protocol.[15]

Since its inception, the Montreal Protocol's Implementation Committee has taken an active role in assisting in the supervision of procedural (e.g. reporting) as well as substantive obligations contained in the Protocol. By June 2016, its work had ultimately led to no less than 72 non-compliance decisions made by the MOP on the basis of Implementation Committee recommendations.[16] Consonant with its mandate to engage primarily in a collegial and facilitative fashion, the Implementation Committee has sought, where possible, to reach for incentive measures to encourage or induce a contracting party back into compliance. To this end, the establishment of a financial mechanism under the aegis of the Montreal Protocol, notably via the Multilateral Fund,[17] has been of crucial importance particularly with regard to developing countries often facing significant resource-related problems to secure implementation of their Protocol obligations. With contracting party contributions totalling €3.7 billion, the Fund has assisted in the underwriting of some 6,000 projects covering all developing countries. Article 5 of the Protocol grants special dispensations to developing country parties in meeting their obligations, including additional time granted to phase-out production and consumption of controlled ozone depleting substances (ODS). Typically, when recommending the distribution of financial assistance, the Implementation Committee has requested or negotiated in return compliance action plans from the contracting parties concerned and performance is always monitored and reviewed at subsequent committee sessions.

Famously, the lever of financial assistance proved reportedly pivotal in resolving Russian non-compliance with certain ODS phase-out requirements in 1995.[18] Where a contracting party fails to demonstrate to the Implementation Committee that appropriate action is being taken to address a situation of non-compliance, for instance over the failure to report on ODS production or consumption data or on the phase-out of certain controlled substances, the Implementation Committee may then typically begin to tighten the screw by cautioning the contracting party concerned that the MOP reserves the right to withdraw access to funding or other assistance and/or take measures to suspend its rights and privileges (such as suspending rights connected with industrial rationalisation[19] of or trade in ODS with a defaulting contracting party[20]). Several cautions have been issued to contracting parties[21] from the Implementation Committee. However, to date these have very rarely materialised into the adoption of harder measures, such as the suspension of rights or privileges.[22] The fact that overall compliance with the Montreal Protocol has been very high (98%) amongst its global membership[23] and that scientific reports have appraised that depletion of ozone layer is on course to be remedied by around the middle of this century[24] are key factors that have contributed towards underpinning the credibility of the non-compliance procedure adopted under the aegis of Montreal Protocol and establishing it as a benchmark against which others have been measured.

1997 Kyoto Protocol Compliance Committee

One of the strongest forms of non-compliance procedure of MEA obligations was the one established to oversee the implementation of the 1997 Kyoto Protocol[25] to the 1992 UN Framework Convention on Climate Change.[26] The Kyoto non-compliance mechanism, whose legal basis was founded on Article 18 of the Protocol, was adopted by the MOP in 2001.[27] However, its operation was delayed until the Protocol's entry into force in 2005.

The Kyoto Protocol KP97 was adopted in order to crystallise specific emissions reductions and limits on developed countries (listed in Annex I of the 1992 Framework Convention), reflecting the emphasis of responsibility placed such countries for taking measures to combat climate change under the 1992 UN Framework Convention on Climate Change. Specifically, Kyoto initially imposed an obligation on Annex I-listed parties to achieve an average reduction of greenhouse gas (GHG) emission levels of 5% as compared with 1990 levels, each country having individualised reduction commitments, by the end of 2012[28] (the first commitment period regarding quantified emissions limitation and reduction). A second commitment period was agreed at the Conference of the Meeting of the Parties in Doha in 2011[29] to extend the application of Kyoto to cover the period 2013–2020. As a result of a long-standing refusal by certain countries, notably the US, to accept the approach of excluding developing countries from being required to undertake GHG emission reductions, the Kyoto Protocol is now set to be superseded by the 2015 Paris Agreement in 2020 as the principal legal instrument driving the international climate change agenda. Notwithstanding its star is fading on the international scene from the perspective of climate change policy, the Kyoto Protocol remains a site of key interest in terms of the evolution of non-compliance procedures for MEAs. In many respects the Kyoto Protocol represents a high-water mark in terms of international interest in non-compliance procedures, in the sense that the mechanism forged under this instrument has been vested with a considerable degree of supervisory capabilities and remains a key reference point for that reason.

The Kyoto Protocol's Compliance Committee, which convened for the first time in 2006, constitutes the institutional heart of the Protocol's non-compliance mechanism. Whilst in broad terms the Kyoto non-compliance procedure shares a number of the same general basic characteristics and objectives as that deployed by the 1987 Montreal Protocol (notably to promote a facilitative approach towards compliance where possible), in several respects it reflects an attempt to establish a far more sophisticated and rigorous 'rule of law' based system with which to hold contracting parties to account over implementation of their obligations. The enhanced degree of sophistication is illustrated by the various ways in which the non-compliance procedure may be triggered, namely: (1) by any contracting party, (2) the Protocol's Secretariat or (3) expert review teams commissioned under Article 8 of the Kyoto Protocol to appraise annual GHG emission inventories, as required to be reported by the individual parties.[30]

Composed of 20 members appointed on the basis of expertise and equitable geographical representation, the Kyoto Compliance Committee is essentially composed of a plenary body which is subdivided into two main branches, namely the facilitative and enforcement branches. The facilitative branch, whose remit is to provide advice and assistance with a view to promoting compliance,[31] has essentially a preventative type role in minimising instances of non-compliance arising, such as providing early warnings to Annex I-listed contracting parties which the branch assesses to be in danger of falling foul of GHG emissions reduction requirements and having the power to recommend mobilisation of technical and financial assistance to assist with implementation of the Protocol's requirements.[32] In contrast, the enforcement branch has a harder-edged role, vested with certain powers to hold contracting parties to account for instances of non-compliance. Specifically, its remit to determine whether, in light of evidence referred to it, a contracting party listed in Annex I has failed to honour its emissions reduction targets, methodological and reporting requirements on GHG emissions or eligibility requirements to participate in flexibility (market) mechanisms foreseen under the Protocol (i.e. the clean development mechanism, joint implementation or emissions trading).[33] If the enforcement branch determines that a party is in non-compliance then it is required to take a range of response measures, some of which are punitive in nature. Notably, where it finds that an Annex I-listed contracting party has failed to adhere to its emissions reduction requirements the enforcement branch must require that party to make up the emissions reduction deficit as well as an additional deduction of 30% in the second commitment period. Where the branch finds non-compliance regarding eligibility requirements for participation in the Protocol's flexibility mechanisms, it is required to suspend the defaulting contracting party's eligibility to participate in these schemes.[34]

The Kyoto Protocol Compliance Committee mechanism constitutes one of the most prescriptive and punitive amongst non-compliance procedures established by MEAs and such a deterrent-based model has not been replicated since.[35] This is further exemplified by the fact that the Committee's enforcement branch, unlike other MEA non-compliance supervisory entities, is empowered to take binding decisions in respect of non-compliance as opposed to being limited to making recommendations to the MOP. Having said that, a three quarters majority of members reflecting a double-majority of Annex I and non-Annex I contracting parties is required in order for a Committee decision to be taken.[36] Appeals to the MOP are also ruled out, with the exception of a possibility for a contracting party to appeal against decisions which make a finding that an assignment of emissions reduction requirements has been exceeded[37] on grounds of denial of due process.[38]

Whilst Article 18 of the Kyoto Protocol stipulates that a formal amendment to the Protocol has to be adopted where the non-compliance procedure entails binding consequences, this has never been carried out. Potentially, this formal legal requirement could have thrown a spanner in the works and further delayed or even hobbled the operations of the Compliance Committee's enforcement branch. However, it appears that in practice contracting parties accepted the legitimacy of the non-compliance mechanism without the need to complete the formal amendment process. The Kyoto Protocol's Compliance Committee system has been active since it came into operation, particularly through the activities of its enforcement branch.[39] By the end of 2015, the enforcement branch had issued non-compliance decisions concerning nine CPs.[40] The majority of these decisions concerned breaches of provisions requiring the establishment of systems to estimate national GHG emissions and sinks. In the cases where the enforcement branch made an adverse finding against a contracting party, the response measures adopted *vis-à-vis* the party concerned included a declaration of non-compliance, a requirement to deliver a compliance plan within three months and suspension from participation in the Protocol's flexibility mechanisms. In every case the non-compliant party satisfied the enforcement branch within a year of its return to compliance.

The Århus Convention Compliance Committee

A third notable and distinct example of a non-compliance procedure being established as part of the fabric of an MEA is the Compliance Committee system relating to the 1998 UNECE Convention on Access to Information, Public Participation in Decision-Making and Access to Justice in Environmental Matters (Århus Convention).[41] Entering into force in 2001, the Århus Convention represents an important milestone in applying internationally acknowledged and accepted principles in favour of enhancing public participation in environmental decision-making, as enunciated in Principle 10 of the 1992 Rio Declaration.[42] Specifically, the regional international agreement requires contracting parties to grant three basic participatory rights to individuals for the purpose of realising a clean environment (the so-called three Århus Convention pillars) namely, a right of access to environmental information,[43] a right to participate in decisions affecting the environment[44] and a right of access to justice in environmental matters.[45] Whilst originally intended to be predominantly regionally focused (namely on the UNECE area) the Århus Convention's political significance has grown internationally as the leading benchmark for application of the Rio Declaration's public participation principles, its membership having expanded from originally 35 signatories to currently 47 contracting parties, some of which lie beyond the European region and within Eurasia or Central Asia.[46] Aside from the EU, which has adopted a range of legislative instruments to establish public participation rights applicable within its own legal order, the Århus Convention remains the central source of international environmental law and guidance regarding guarantees for civil society's rights to engage in shaping the development and supervising the application of environmental policy.

Article 15 of the Århus Convention provides the legal basis for the establishment of a non-compliance procedure for managing disputes regarding application of the MEA. It stipulates that contracting parties set up on consensual basis optional non-confrontational, non-judicial and consultative arrangements for reviewing compliance, also allowing 'appropriate' public involvement and with the option of admitting communications from members of the public. The decision to require public involvement in compliance review matters constituted a ground-breaking step to implement Principle 10 of the 1992 Rio Declaration at international level. Hitherto, MEAs which had erected non-compliance procedures had foreseen only contracting parties (states and, where relevant, regional economic international organisations such as the EU) to be involved in the operation of such procedures.

The Århus Convention's non-compliance procedure was established formally in 2002 at the first COP,[47] with a central Compliance Committee envisaged to oversee supervisory work. Public involvement constitutes a strong theme underpinning the Committee's operations. Composed of nine members elected by contracting parties or signatories, nominations for committee posts may be made by environmental NGOs in addition to states, another innovative feature. Compliance Committee members serve in their capacity as independent experts, as opposed to the standard role of state representative used in several MEAs.[48] Significantly, the non-compliance procedure specifically allows communications from the public to trigger the compliance review process, alongside the more standard and predictable triggers of contracting party submissions and referrals from the Convention's Secretariat. Similar to the non-compliance mechanism deployed under the aegis of the 1987 Montreal Protocol, the Århus Convention vests the MOP (in light of Compliance Committee recommendations) with power to decide upon a range of measures in response to instances of non-compliance, including: the provision of advice and assistance; making recommendations; requesting the submission of a compliance plan; issuing declarations of non-compliance and/or cautions; as well as suspending rights and privileges.[49]

In practice, the bulk of the work of the Århus Convention's Compliance Committee has been serviced by communications from the public concerning complaints about non-compliance concerning the three pillars relating to access to information, public participation in decision-making or access to environmental justice. By end of March 2018, the Århus Convention's Compliance Committee had received 157 communications from the public[50] (with 46 being found by the Committee to be inadmissible). In contrast, other trigger mechanisms have been barely used. No contracting party had referred itself to the Compliance Committee (so-called self-trigger) and there had been no referrals from the Secretariat of the Convention either. Only three contracting parties had made submissions to the Committee, one requesting legal interpretative advice[51] and two others filing complaints about another party's shortcomings relating to public participation in environmental decision-making (party-to-party trigger).[52] The MOP to the Århus Convention had made 42 decisions concerning non-compliance by end of 2017.[53] Consonant with its facilitative and non-confrontational approach, the MOP has so far made little use of the range of sharper-edged response measures in its locker. Specifically, there have been no decisions suspending rights or privileges and only three contracting parties have received a caution as a result of persistent non-compliance.[54] Typically, the approach of the MOP has been to request a non-compliant contracting party to provide information, undertake action to return to compliance and/or report back by a certain deadline.

Evaluation of non-compliance procedures in MEAs

Since the establishment of the 1987 Montreal Protocol's non-compliance procedural mechanism in 1990, several other MEAs have set up or otherwise enhanced their own collective non-compliance review procedures.[55] There is no doubt that these systems have flourished and become a constituent supervisory element of a considerable number of international and regional environmental accords, and they have received general endorsement from the UN.[56] However, as noted by Klabbers,[57] it is a challenging task to assess their effectiveness. In particular, it is impossible to know with certainty what precise impact they have made in terms of enhancing compliance. Moreover, each MEA is subject to particular political dynamics, objectives and priorities for contracting parties that materially affect the prospects for and shape of any collective non-compliance procedure negotiated between the parties.[58] The unique features of each international environmental accord make it acutely difficult to craft a uniform approach regarding the development of non-compliance procedural mechanisms.[59] Ultimately, much depends on the degree of conscientiousness amongst contracting parties over adherence to their MEA obligations.[60] However, various factors and perspectives may be usefully considered for analysing the extent to which non-compliance procedures are in general likely to influence contracting party behaviour positively in respect of properly implementing their international environmental obligations.

As has been widely acknowledged, multilateral non-compliance procedures have several general features in common that make them attractive as a means of complementing the traditional, formal mechanisms of inter-state dispute settlement principles and procedures existing in international environmental law and treaty practice.[61] Their collectivist nature and outlook assists in ensuring that MEA objectives as opposed to domestic internal interests of states are the focus of action to supervise compliance. The non-compliance procedural process resonates here with the reality that states are as likely to be victim as villain in the context of MEAs addressing global environmental problems.[62] The facilitative nature and outlook of such collective dispute resolution procedures also brings with it substantial advantages. The fact that non-compliance procedures seek to promote full compliance over a period of time, particularly using advice and assistance as measures of first resort, as opposed to punishing individual instances of non-compliance, is arguably more likely to galvanise statal support and build collective trust. In being able usually to use a wide range of response tools (from advice and assistance through to suspension of rights and privileges) non-compliance procedural systems have the benefit also of being capable of attuning themselves to the particular context and circumstances of individual non-compliance scenarios.

Notably, where non-compliance procedures are able to provide financial and/or technical assistance, this has proved to be particularly invaluable for addressing capacity issues facing many developing countries and also reflects and seeks to implement the cardinal principle of common but differentiated responsibility, woven into the fabric of contemporary IEL as underscored by the 1992 Rio Declaration.[63] For example, the opening up of access to funding from the Global Environment Facility and provision of training and information workshops in relation to the 2000 Biosafety Protocol[64] to the Convention on Biological Diversity has been noted by that MEA's compliance committee as having led to a substantial increase in contracting parties submitting national implementation reports. Only 35% of contracting parties had submitted their first implementation reports by the set deadline of 2007, when no financial assistance had been made available to assisting developing countries regarding their completion. However, the submission rate had risen to 89% in respect of the second implementation report required to be submitted in 2011 and 62% in respect of the third implementation report due by the end of 2015; access to supportive funding for developing countries had become available regarding both of these reporting rounds.[65] The emphasis on assistance as a primary non-compliance procedural device or response tool resonates strongly with the managerialist school of thought, which considers that lack of capacity constitutes a key factor of non-compliance with MEAs.[66]

Other key advantages of collective non-compliance procedures are their preventative[67] as well as prospective or forward-looking[68] approaches regarding the issue of adherence to environmental treaty obligations. They are intended to underpin across the MEA membership monitoring, verification and implementation provisions and obligations. In contrast to the general international legal principle of state responsibility, the existence of an 'injured' state is not required for the operation of non-compliance procedures. In addition, the informality, non-confrontational nature and relative flexibility of non-compliance procedural systems are attractive features for a number of reasons. Notably, non-compliance issues may be addressed relatively quickly and regularly, so focusing on ongoing as opposed to historic breaches. Moreover, where the possibility exists for a non-party to trigger the procedural process (e.g. such as a treaty secretariat or members of the public as in the case of the 1998 Århus Convention), there is far less chance for diplomatic relationships between states to be undermined or to interfere with the compliance review process.

It is clear, though, that non-compliance procedures do not automatically constitute a magic bullet for ensuring compliance with MEAs. Ultimately, they can but provide incentives (weak or strong depending on the range and nature of sanction underpinning them) for states to ensure adherence to their international environmental protection obligations. Such dispute resolution systems are not vested with any powers to ensure that enforcement is actually achieved within the territories of contracting parties. Moreover, they are usually essentially reliant upon contracting parties to provide them with information on the state of treaty implementation in the form of national reports. States are, in the main, unwilling to vest international bodies with powers of independent inspection and monitoring. However, if appropriately equipped with the necessary legal, administrative and financial resources, non-compliance procedures may be capable of exerting a marked influence on the degree to which contracting parties take steps to comply with their MEA obligations.

Those MEA non-compliance procedures which are heavily or wholly reliant upon facilitative response tools risk being overly dependent upon the assumed goodwill of contracting parties to comply with their international obligations (in accordance with the general kernel international legal principle that recognises a basic duty incumbent on states to fulfilment their international contractual obligations, *pacta sunt servanda* [69]). As has been pointed out elsewhere, a risk associated with non-compliance procedural mechanisms is that they may serve to compromise on upholding the role of law in favour of a set of long-term objectives.[70] This appears evident, in particular, where procedural structures do not dispose of response measures that may serve to place real pressure on persistently defaulting contracting parties to take remedial action to bring them into a state of compliance.[71]

The 1979 Convention on Long-Range Transboundary Air Pollution[72] (CLRTAP) provides a case in point.[73] For the non-compliance procedure established under that MEA's regime since 1998 does not envisage the deployment of any measures designed to place significant pressure on a non-compliant contracting party, such as suspension or treaty rights or privileges.[74] It has little in the way of meaningful responses to offer in the face of persistent offending and is effectively reliant on the voluntary compliance of states. This absence of any potential punitive dimension to the non-compliance procedural system undermines the deterrent value of the MEA and its ability to address the phenomenon of serious or persistent offending. The lack of teeth in armoury of response measures was with little doubt a significant factor underlying the failure by Spain and Greece for some 14 years each to comply with certain air emission reduction obligations, notwithstanding those parties being on the receiving end of several non-compliance decisions from the Convention's Executive Body.[75]

Moreover, non-compliance procedures appear considerably less active and effective where there is no possibility for their processes to be triggered by a non-party, such as the treaty's secretariat or the public,[76] for states are usually most reluctant to trigger non-compliance procedures against other fellow state parties. This is understandable given the risk of a party-to-party trigger undermining diplomatic relations or fear of it giving rise to retaliatory responses. The absence of an independent trigger to the non-compliance procedure[77] underpinning the 1996 London Protocol to the Marine Dumping Convention[78] has, with little doubt, significantly hampered efforts to increase the number of national reports on implementation and monitoring, which are required by that international instrument to be submitted annually.[79] In 2011, steps were taken under the 1989 UN Basel Convention on the Control of the Transboundary Movements of Hazardous Waste and their Disposal[80] so as to broaden the treaty secretariat's powers so as to empower it to make referrals to the MEA's Implementation Committee beyond the area of reporting obligations.[81] In part, this was a reaction to the fact that, hitherto, no contracting party had made use of the non-compliance procedure to address issues relating to substantive non-compliance.[82]

Other key factors likely to have a significant bearing on the degree of effectiveness of non-compliance procedures include the related aspects of transparency and public involvement. The greater degree to which non-compliance review systems are made public will assist in placing greater pressure on contracting parties to adhere to their environmental treaty obligations. Likewise, the greater degree of participatory rights accorded to civil society (including, in particular, NGOs) in the review process will open up new sources of information and scrutiny regarding non-compliance issues. With only a few exceptions, such as CITES and the Århus Convention,[83] currently MEAs offer relatively little meaningful opportunity for public participation in non-compliance procedural systems.

One other key factor to note regarding the relative effectiveness of non-compliance procedures is the degree to which they are able to coexist satisfactorily with traditional inter-state dispute settlement procedures, which are typically provided for in the same agreement. Several MEAs clarify that their non-compliance procedures are to operate without prejudice to other dispute resolution systems contained within the treaty framework, but this has not been specified or otherwise made clear in all agreements, and a number of legal questions remain as yet unanswered as to what impact (if any) recourse to a non-compliance procedure may have on the availability of other dispute settlement procedures, and *vice versa.*[84]

Notwithstanding the steady increase in number of collective non-compliance procedures amongst the collection of (global) MEAs, the inclusion of more classical (binary) dispute settlement provisions retains important attractions and relevance for states. This is particularly pertinent in the context of MEAs with strong bilateral features, namely agreements which affect relations and/or transactions between individual states (such as agreements imposing controls on the transnational trade in substances or species).[85] In the context of such inter-statal disputes, recourse to traditional dispute settlement procedures may well be far more attractive to the claimant state in terms of being able to lever an appropriate remedy under general principles of state responsibility.[86] In contrast, collective non-compliance systems are likely to be more appropriate fora for the purpose of addressing non-compliance matters affecting the global or a regional community at large, as opposed to specific states.

Notes

1 See Cardesa-Salzmann (2011) at 104.
2 See e.g. Wettestad (2007) at 975 and Dupuy/Vinuales (2015) in Chapter 8, especially at 237–243.

3 Examples include the 1971 Ramsar Convention (996 U.N.T.S.245), 1972 World Heritage Convention (1037 U.N.T.S.151) and 1979 Bonn Convention on the Migratory Species of Wild Animals (19 ILM 15 (1980)).
4 Examples include the 1985 Vienna Ozone Layer Convention (26 ILM 1529 (1985)), 1992 UN Framework Convention on Climate Change (1771 U.N.T.S.107) and 1992 Convention on Biological Diversity (31 ILM 822 (1992)).
5 Examples include the 1979 Convention on Long Range Transboundary Air Pollution (CLRTAP) (18 ILM 1442 (1979)), 1987 Montreal Protocol on Substances that Deplete the Ozone Layer (26 ILM 54 (1987)), 1989 Basel Convention on the Control of the Transboundary Movements of Hazardous Waste and their Disposal (28 ILM 657 (1989)), 1996 London Protocol to the Convention on Prevention of Marine Pollution by Dumping of Wastes and Other Matter (36 ILM 1 (1997)), 1997 Kyoto Protocol to the United Nations Framework Convention on Climate Change (37 ILM 22 (1998)), 2000 Cartagena Biosafety Protocol to the Convention on Biological Diversity (39 ILM 1027 (2000)) and 2001 International Treaty on Plant Genetic Resources for Food and Agriculture (IT-PGRFA) (www.planttreaty.org).
6 UNEP *Guidelines on Compliance and Enforcement of Multilateral Environmental Agreements* (UNEP, SS.VII/4, 4.2.2002).
7 Para. 14(d), ibid.
8 26 ILM 154 (1987).
9 26 ILM 1529 (1985).
10 1973 Washington Convention on International Trade in Endangered Species (983 U.N.T.S. 243 (1973)).
11 In 2000 a formal and general multilateral non-compliance procedure was introduced for CITES Resolution 11.3 (Rev. CoP-16) with accompanying procedural guidance agreed to in 2007 (Resolution 14.3). For comments on the distinctive compliance system under CITES, see e.g. Biniaz (2006) 89 and Sand (2013) 259.
12 By virtue of the Kigali Amendment, adopted by the MOP-28 in 2016 and set to enter into force on 1 January 2019, Montreal Protocol parties are required to gradually reduce HFC use by 80–85% by the late 2040s, anticipated to avoid up to 0.5 degree Celsius of global temperature rise by 2100. http://ozone.unep.org/en/handbook-montreal-protocol-substances-deplete-ozone-layer/41453
13 Decision IV/5 of MOP-4 (1992).
14 Decision X/10 of MOP-10 (1998).
15 See Annex V to Decision IV/5 of MOP-4.
16 See decisions listed in the online *Handbook for the Montreal Protocol* 10th ed (2016) available for inspection on the Montreal Protocol website at: http://ozone.unep.org/en/handbook-montreal-protocol-substances-deplete-ozone-layer/25411
17 See: http://www.multilateralfund.org/default.aspx
18 See Decision VII/18 MOP-7, as appraised by e.g. Adsett/Daniel/Husain/McDorman (2004) at 119.
19 See e.g. Art.2(5) and 2(5*bis*) of the 1987 Montreal Protocol which provide for the transfer of production and consumption rights for controlled ODS.
20 Art.4 of the Montreal Protocol prohibits contracting parties from trading in ODS with non-parties, which includes other contacting parties whose rights under Art.4 are suspended.

21 The author has calculated from Montreal Protocol's Implementation Committee reports that over 100 cautions have been issued by the Committee as at the time of writing in June 2016.
22 In Decision XVII/26 (2005) the MOP requested exporting contracting parties to assist Azerbaijan implement its requirement to ban importing Annex A group I controlled ODS (CFCs) by ceasing export of those ODS to Azerbaijan, whilst stopping short of imposing a formal trade suspension decision. That MOP decision followed several others, which made note of a contracting party's non-compliance with phasing-out CFCs (Decisions X/20, XV/28 and XVI/21).
23 As at April 2018, there were 197 contracting parties to the Montreal Protocol. See Montreal Protocol website at: http://ozone.unep.org/sites/ozone/modules/unep/ozone_treaties/inc/datasheet.php
24 See e.g. Solomon/ Ivy/Kinnison/ Mills/Neely/Schmidt (2016).
25 38 ILM 517 (1998).
26 1771 U.N.T.S.107 (1992).
27 Decision 24/CP.7 COP-MOP1. See Yoshida (2011) at 41.
28 Art. 3(1) in conjunction with Annex B of the 1997 Kyoto Protocol.
29 The so-called Doha Amendment agreed at CMP-18.
30 Decision 24/CP.7 paras. VI and VIII.
31 Para. IV, ibid.
32 Para. XIV, ibid.
33 Para. V, ibid.
34 Para. XV, ibid.
35 Indeed, the recent 2015 Paris Agreement to the UN Framework Convention on Climate Change (C.N.92.2016.TREATIES-XXVII.7.d), which is due to succeed the 1997 Kyoto Protocol in 2020, provides that its compliance committee mechanism is to be 'facilitative in nature in a manner that is transparent, non-adversarial and non-punitive' (Art.15(2) Paris Agreement).
36 Para. II(9) of Decision 24/CP.7 COP-MOP1.
37 Namely, a finding of a breach of Art.3(1) of the 1997 Kyoto Protocol.
38 Para. XI of Decision 24/CP.7 COP-MOP1.
39 Whilst the facilitative branch has considered early warning issues in respect of four contracting parties (Austria, Canada, Croatia and Italy) it ultimately decided that three were on track to meet their GHG emission reduction obligations for the first commitment period, whilst Canada's situation was affected by its withdrawal from the Protocol as from 15 December 2012.
40 Enforcement branch decisions have been made in respect of the following contracting parties: Greece (2008), Canada (2008), Croatia (2009), Bulgaria (2010), Romania (2011), Ukraine (2011), Lithuania (2011), Slovakia (2012) and Monaco (2014). Summaries of the enforcement branch's decisions are provided in the Kyoto Protocol's Information Notes which are published online by the Kyoto Protocol Secretariat, available at: http://unfccc.int/kyoto_protocol/compliance/items/2875.php
41 38 ILM 517 (1999). See e.g. Jendrośka (2011), Kravchenko (2007), Koester (2007) and, more generally on the Convention, Pallemaerts (2011).
42 UN Doc. A/CONF.151/26/Rev1. Specifically, Principle 10 of the Rio Declaration states:

> 'Environmental issues are best handled with the participation of all concerned citizens, at the relevant level. At the national level, each individual shall have appropriate access to information concerning the environment that is held by public authorities, including information on hazardous materials and activities in their communities, and the opportunity to participate in decision-making processes. States shall facilitate and encourage public awareness and participation by making information widely available. Effective access to judicial and administrative proceedings, including redress and remedy, shall be provided.'

43 See Arts.4–5 Århus Convention.
44 See Arts.6–8, ibid.
45 See Art.9, ibid.
46 Namely, Azerbaijan, Kazakhstan, Kyrgyzstan, Tajikistan and Turkmenistan.
47 Decision I/7 *Review of Compliance* COP-1.
48 See para. I.2 of Decision I/7 which states that committee members 'shall be persons of high moral character and recognized competence in the fields to which the Convention relates, including persons having legal experience.'
49 Para. XII, ibid.
50 Information concerning Communications from the public to the Århus Convention Compliance Committee is available on the relevant UNECE website at: http://www.unece.org/env/pp/cc/com.html
51 Belarus ACCC/A/2014/1.
52 *Romania v Ukraine (Bystre Canal Project)* ACCC/S/2004/1 and *Lithuania v Belarus (Nuclear Power project)* ACCC/S/2015/2.
53 Decisions taken by the MOP of the Århus Convention regarding non-compliance may be inspected at: http://www.unece.org/env/pp/mop.html
54 Ukraine, Kazakhstan and Turkmenistan.
55 For an overview, see, e.g., UNEP, *Compliance Mechanisms Under Selected Multilateral Agreements* (UNEP 2007). For an indicative list of MEAs currently deploying non-compliance procedures, see note 5. Negotiations are currently pending regarding the establishment of non-compliance procedures for other MEAs, including notably the 1998 Rotterdam Convention (38 ILM 1 (1998)) and 2001 Stockholm (POPs) Convention (40 ILM 532 (2001)).
56 See 2002 UNEP *Guidelines on Compliance and Enforcement of Multilateral Environmental Agreements* (UNEP, SS.VII/4, 4.2.2002) and 2003 UNECE *Guidelines for Strengthening Compliance and Implementation of Multilateral Environmental Agreements in the ECE Region* (ECE/CEP/107).
57 Klabbers (2007) at 1004.
58 Goteyn (2011) at 794.
59 See e.g. the appraisal of the European Commission of the EU on this matter in SEC (2005)405 *Staff Working Paper on Compliance Mechanisms in MEAs*, 18.3.2005.
60 Marauhn (1996).
61 See e.g. Boyle (1991) at 230 and Bodansky (2010) at 248.
62 See Brunnée (2005) at 8.
63 See notably Principle 7 of the Rio Declaration (UN Doc. A/CONF.151/26/Rev1).

64 39 ILM 1027 (2000).

65 Biosafety Protocol Compliance Committee Report, *Review of Compliance with the Obligation to Submit National Reports and Whether the Information in the Reports Is Complete* (20.1.2016): UNEP/CBD/BS/CC/13/2.

66 See e.g. Neumayer (2012) at 11.

67 See e.g. Fitzmaurice/Redgwell (2000) at 40.

68 Bodansky (2010) at 248.

69 See e.g. Brownlie (1990) at 616, Thirlway (2003) at 117 *et seq*. See also Art.26 VCLT.

70 See Klabbers (2007) at 1007 and Goteyn/Maes (2011) at 824.

71 See O'Connell (1995) at 56.

72 18 ILM 1442 (1979).

73 Adsett/Daniel/Husain/McDorman (2004) at 126.

74 See Decision 2012/25 *On Improving the Functioning of the Implementation Committee* at para. XII (Consideration by the Executive Body). Under this provision the CLRTAP Executive Body may decide upon measures of a non-discriminatory nature to bring about full compliance, including assistance and any such decision must be taken by consensus.

75 Spain received nine non-compliance decisions over its failure between 1999–2013 to comply with its emission reduction obligations concerning volatile organic compounds (VOCs) under the 1991 Geneva Protocol to CLRTAP (31 ILM 568 (1992)). Greece received ten non-compliance decisions over its failure between 1997–2013 to comply with its nitrous oxide (NOx) reduction obligations as required by the 1988 Sofia Protocol to CLRTAP (28 ILM 214 (1988)). Data on non-compliance decisions gleaned from the CLRTAP website at: http://www.unece.org/env/lrtap/executive body/eb_decision.html

76 See e.g. Cardesa-Salzmann (2011) at 122.

77 LC 29/17 Annex 7 (2007).

78 36 ILM 1 (1997).

79 See the *Report of the 8th Meeting of the Compliance Group under the London Protocol* (LC37/WP.2, 9.10.2015) in which the Protocol's Compliance Group conceded that it had no clear knowledge of the reasons for the downward trend in national reporting. The Compliance Group noted that only 12 reports had ever been submitted on implementing measures (out of a membership of 47 contracting parties).

80 28 ILM 657 (1989).

81 Decision BC-10/11 COP-10.

82 UNEP, *The Basel Mechanism for Promoting Implementation and Compliance: Celebrating a Decade of Assistance to Parties* (UNEP 2011) at 7.

83 Notably, the 1998 Århus Convention (38 ILM 517 (1999)) and CITES (983 U.N.T.S. 243 (1973)). Under CITES independent reviews of trade in species are carried out by the TRAFFIC monitoring network for the CITES Secretariat and CPs (a network with strong links to environmental NGOs, notably IUCN and WWF). It should also be noted that where a MEA regime provides the possibility for one of its institutions to trigger a compliance review mechanism, this constitutes an indirect opportunity for NGOs and other members of the public to provide information to the international institution with a view to persuading it to commencing the relevant non-compliance procedure.

84 See Klabbers (2007) at 1006; Sands (2006) at 353.
85 Examples of such MEAs include the 1989 UN Basel Convention on Control of Transboundary Movements of Hazardous Waste (28 ILM 657 (1989)), the 1998 UN Rotterdam Convention on the Prior Informed Consent procedure for certain Hazardous Chemicals and Pesticides in International Trade (38 ILM 1 (1999)) and the 2000 UN Biosafety Protocol to the Convention on Biological Diversity (39 ILM 1027 (2000)).
86 See e.g. comments by Cardesa-Salzmann (2011) at 118.

6 The European Union's special enforcement mechanisms

In analysing systems developed at international level for the purpose of enhancing enforcement of international environmental obligations, it is useful to take stock of the unique features of the European Union's supranational legal order. It is important not to discount the impact of the EU in terms of analysis and discussion regarding the enforcement of international environmental obligations, as the Union forms part of the web of international organisations and legal systems that collectively contribute towards enhancing international level co-operation on the environment. Whilst the EU does have some unusual legal and governance features (as will be commented on in this chapter) amongst international regimes that concern themselves with the environment sector, it is still at root a set of international agreements amongst independent national states and constitutes ultimately a source of regional international law[1] and accordingly may be said to constitute part of the broader family of international co-operative arrangements on environmental protection that collectively form the subject of IEL. The EU's system of supervising implementation of its environmental protection norms is considerably more assertive than the relatively soft manner of MEA engagement in law enforcement issues generally experienced at international level and is therefore worthy of particular scrutiny.

The EU, usually referred to in international organisational discourse rather misleadingly as a regional economic integration organisation (REIO),[2] first started to develop a common environmental protection programme in the early 1970s.[3] Ever since the amendments introduced to its founding treaty framework by virtue of 1986 Single European Act,[4] the Union's constitutional framework has formally incorporated and subsequently further entrenched a common environmental protection policy as an integral part of its activities, requiring the realisation of its internal market to be consonant with 'the sustainable development of Europe' and based on a 'high level of protection and improvement of the quality of the environment'.[5] The Union's current founding treaty framework[6] anchors the EU's environmental policy to the principles of precaution, preventive action, proximity and polluter pays,[7] whilst also stipulating that environmental protection requirements must be integrated into the definition and implementation of Union policies and activities.[8] From an international perspective, the EU's environmental policy competences provide the regional organisation with a broad mandate to engage actively with the international community with a view to addressing specifically include global environmental protection issues. Specifically, Article 191 of the Treaty on the Functioning of the EU (TFEU) includes the requirement that Union environmental policy shall contribute to 'the promotion of international level to deal with regional or worldwide problems, and in particular climate change'. The EU's Charter of Fundamental Rights,[9] a constituent part of the Union's contemporary constitutional legal framework since 1 December 2009,[10] requires the Union to ensure that a high level of environmental protection and improvement to environmental quality are integrated within EU policies and ensured in accordance with the principle of sustainable development.[11] These legal foundations have underpinned the adoption of some 200 pieces of EU legislation across a wide range of environmental topic areas, including notably in relation to the water, waste, air quality, climate change, nature and chemicals management sectors. The European Commission, the Union's principal executive institution, has assessed that these measures constitute the bedrock of much of the national environmental policies across the EU's member states, estimating that some 80% of environmental laws adopted at the national level in the Union are based upon EU environmental legislation.[12]

As far as the enforcement of its environmental norms are concerned, the EU counts as having perhaps the strongest set of legal tools at its disposal amongst international treaties concerning environmental protection.[13] The Union has developed its legal system to ensure that law enforcement is assisted both supranational as well as national levels (so centrally as well as decentralised) in three principal ways: namely, by EU institutions, by civil society as well by national authorities of the constituent member states. Each of these three aspects will be addressed briefly in turn.

Centralised enforcement of EU environmental law

From its inception, the EU has provided for a distinctively robust centralised supranational institutional role in law enforcement. The

Union charges two of its institutions with responsibility to ensure the proper application of EU rules, namely the European Commission (hereafter referred to as the 'Commission') and Court of Justice of the EU (CJEU). Specifically, under the Union's treaty framework, whilst the Commission is charged with a general responsibility to 'ensure the application of the Treaties, and of measures adopted by the institutions pursuant to them' and 'oversee the application of Union law under the control of the Court of Justice of the European Union',[14] the CJEU is vested with the task of ensuring that 'in the interpretation and application of the Treaties the law is observed'.[15]

The Commission is empowered to bring before the CJEU legal proceedings against member states that have breached EU law. Such legal action is commonly referred to as infringement or infraction proceedings.[16] Somewhat resonant with the facilitative approach adopted by collective compliance mechanisms developed at international level (discussed in Chapter 5), the Commission first liaises with the member state concerned to seek an amicable resolution out of court, where at all possible. Whilst originally the EU legal framework only foresaw the possibility of the CJEU issuing a judicial declaration of non-compliance, by virtue of treaty amendments introduced in 1993 and 2009[17] the CJEU is now vested with additional powers to impose financial penalties on defaulting member states. Specifically, the Court has the power to impose a daily penalty and/or lump sum payment on a member state which it finds guilty of an infringement. These penalties may be imposed either where a member state has failed to notify the Commission of measures to implement a legislative directive,[18] where a member state fails to adhere to an emergency injunction (interim relief order) granted under Article 279 TFEU in respect of a suspected violation of EU law[19] or where a member state has failed to respect a previous CJEU judgment that found it guilty of non-compliance with Union law.[20] The infringement procedures' authority is underlined by EU treaty stipulations affirming the mandatory nature of CJEU jurisdiction; member states are prohibited from submitting disputes regarding the interpretation or application of EU law to dispute settlement procedures other than those provided under the EU founding treaties.[21]

In practice, the Union's infringement procedures have featured as important part of the EU's supervision of member state implementation of EU environmental protection legislation. By the end of 2014, over 550 environmental infringement judgments had been handed down by the CJEU.[22] As of the end of March 2018, 16 out of a total of 29 CJEU judgments (55%) resulting in the imposition of financial penalties on defaulting member states concerned breaches of EU environmental law.[23] The European Commission continues to report the environment sector as being an area that continues to attract a high level of infringement casework.[24]

The infringement procedures have been subject to criticism, including concerning their rather cumbersome and protracted nature,[25] as well as lack of investigative powers[26] and administrative resources[27] vested in the Commission to oversee them. In addition, in recent years the Commission has also pared down its use of the procedures to focus on priority areas it considers to be the most serious instances of non-compliance.[28] Nevertheless, the infringement procedure system continues to feature as a significant component of EU environmental law enforcement machinery and there is little doubt that instances of member state non-compliance would be significantly higher without them.

Decentralised enforcement of EU environmental law

The EU legal system has also developed, through a combination of legislative instrumentation as well as CJEU jurisprudence, possibilities for civil society to participate in law enforcement. The CJEU, through its enunciation and development of a range of unwritten general principles and doctrines of EU law (notably direct and indirect effect, supremacy and state liability)[29] has opened up certain possibilities for individuals to be able to enforce EU environmental legislative provisions before national courts. By way of illustration, in the *Janecek* judgment[30] the CJEU held that individuals had a right as a matter of Union law to seek judicial redress before the national courts in order to enforce a directly effective stipulation contained in a Union legislative instrument on ambient air quality,[31] which requires member states to adopt plans indicating measures to be taken when faced with a risk of EU legislative limit values or alert thresholds on air quality being exceeded. The monist position adopted by the CJEU regarding the penetration of EU law within the domestic legal orders of the member states contrasts markedly with the general position accepted under international law, which assumes that the extent to which individuals may rely directly upon international norms before national courts is a matter for individual national legal orders to determine (in the absence of specific international agreement on the matter).[32]

As a contracting party[33] to the 1998 UNECE Århus Convention on Access to Information, Public Participation in Decision-Making and Access to Justice in Environmental Matters[34] the EU has adopted a number of implementation measures requiring member states to ensure that individuals have access to justice for the purpose of upholding of 'the three pillars' of the Convention. Specifically, the EU has adopted legislation to guarantee individual rights regarding access to environmental information,[35] public participation in environmental decision-making,[36] and (to a limited extent) with respect to the enforcement of EU environmental law.[37] EU legislation has also been adopted in order to enhance access to justice for individuals with respect to EU environmental decision-making, notably via Regulation 1367/2006 (the so-called 'EU Århus Regulation').[38]

These legislative initiatives, whilst unprecedented at international organisational level, have so far fallen short of full implementation of the Århus Convention's third pillar regarding access to environmental justice. As far as facilitating access to environmental justice at EU member state level is concerned, there remain significant gaps in coverage with, for instance, no Union-level access to justice provision in relation to the areas of water, waste and air quality policy. Whilst the Commission proposed a 'horizontal' access to justice instrument in 2003,[39] the draft instrument never received sufficient political support from the member state representatives within the Council of the EU in order to become adopted. In May 2014, the legislative proposal was quietly withdrawn by the Commission,[40] this notwithstanding a seemingly strong commitment made with regard to the enhancement of access to environmental justice contained in the Union's current Seventh Environment Action Programme (EAP7) spanning 2013–2020.[41] Moreover, the current rules on legal standing in relation to EU-level judicial review proceedings,[42] requiring individual plaintiffs to prove that they are both individually as well as directly concerned by a Union measure they wish to challenge (the so-called *Plaumann* test[43]), make it very difficult for individuals to seek annulment of EU measures they suspect of contravening EU environmental protection requirements.[44] A similarly restrictive approach to standing has also been endorsed by the CJEU with respect to the mechanism contained in the EU Århus Regulation allowing NGOs limited rights to request an internal review of EU administrative acts affecting the environment.[45] The current state of EU rules on standing is highly questionable in terms of its compliance with the third pillar requirements of the Århus Convention, the Convention's Compliance Committee having already delivered a critical recommendation in 2011[46] concerning the EU's rules as they stood prior to the amendments introduced by the 2007 Lisbon Treaty. The Århus Compliance Committee, which reserved judgment on the situation applying post-Lisbon, delivered subsequent follow-up recommendation on 17 March 2017[47] in which the Committee found that the EU's current law relating to access to environmental justice in respect of Union-level environmental decision-making violate Article 9(3) and (4) of the Convention. It recommended that the Union either amends the EU Århus Regulation or that the CJEU amends its jurisprudence on legal standing requirements. The EU has yet to ensure that its internal rules on standing are in alignment with Article 9 of the Convention.

As a third string to its bow, the EU has developed a range of legislative and other initiatives to enhance the role national authorities in upholding the proper application of EU environmental law within the member states. Whilst the EU treaty framework acknowledges that Union member states are primarily responsible and competent to ensure due implementation of EU obligations at national level, it also recognises a common interest in ensuring that this is carried out effectively.[48] Notably, the general 'good faith' clause enshrined in the Union's founding treaty framework[49] places a general legal duty on member states to take steps to ensure their compliance with EU obligations as well as to engage in sincere co-operation with the Union for this purpose. Since the early 2000s, the EU has adopted a number of measures with a view to ensuring that national authorities have a minimum range of enforcement tools at their disposal.

With respect to the matter of sanctions, two general EU legislative instruments stand out, namely the 2004 EU Environmental Liability Directive[50] and the 2008 EU Environmental Crimes Directive.[51] Whereas the Environmental Liability Directive obliges member states to ensure that their national competent authorities take steps to hold operators account for instances of significant environmental damage and oversee remediation of damaged sites, the Environmental Crimes Directive obliges member states to penalise serious breaches of EU environmental law through the use of effective, proportionate and dissuasive criminal sanctions.[52] The EU has also adopted other legislative instruments requiring competent authorities to impose financial penalties on operators failing to adhere to its climate change rules: namely, the Emissions Trading Directive[53] as well as the Union's secondary legislation on CO_2 emission performance standards for light-duty vehicles (i.e. passenger cars and light vans).[54] The Emissions Trading Directive requires that member states ensure that operators covered by its terms who fail to surrender sufficient carbon emission allowances by the end of April annually in order to cover their emissions from the previous year pay an excess emissions penalty of €100 per tonne of CO_2 emitted.[55] The EU legislation on CO_2 emissions performance of light-duty vehicles stipulates that a specific 'excess emissions premium' must be paid by an automobile manufacturer to the Commission in the event of the former exceeding the specific auto CO_2 emissions target set for it under the aegis of the Union legislation.[56] Apart from legislative instrumentation on sanctions, the EU has also adopted measures, both general[57] and sectoral,[58] establishing minimum standards concerning environmental inspections carried out by national authorities.[59] Notwithstanding a commitment in EAP7[60] to extend binding criteria for effective national inspections and surveillance, work on developing a comprehensive legal framework via a horizontal legislative instrument appears to have stalled for the time being.

Some brief reflections on the EU's approach to environmental law enforcement

Although the EU has developed by far the most sophisticated and far-reaching law enforcement mechanisms amongst MEA regimes, this does not mean though that the Union's track record of achievement regarding the implementation of its environmental obligations has been necessarily exemplary. For notwithstanding the various pieces of law enforcement machinery in place, there remain serious deficiencies on the part of EU member states in ensuring timely and full compliance with EU environmental legislation. For instance, in 2011 an environmental consultancy study commissioned for the Union estimated that the annual cost of non-implementation of the EU's environmental legislative *acquis* amounted to some €50bn.[61] In March 2015, the EU Network for the Implementation and Enforcement of Environmental Law (IMPEL) published a report[62] signalling general concerns with the state of implementation by member states of a wide range of EU environmental legislative instruments (notably in the water, waste, nature protection, air quality, agricultural and chemical sectors), noting in particular a general lack of resourcing, skills and capacity at the level of national authorities responsible for environmental regulation and enforcement as well as inadequate levels of sanctions to deal with persons breaching EU environmental requirements.

Well aware of these long-standing problems, the European Commission has by way of response launched a new policy initiative (known as the Environmental Implementation Review) in June 2016.[63] The idea behind the EIR is to increase focus on enhancing the state of national implementation of EU environmental law through a range of measures, including publication of periodic country-specific compliance reports and arrangement of high-level discussions on addressing major implementation gaps common to several member states. Notwithstanding shortcomings over implementation, there is little doubt that the various initiatives undertaken at EU level on law enforcement has made a significant contribution towards ensuring that member state compliance performance is considerably higher than that experienced generally amongst MEAs.

Notes

1 See e.g. De Witte (2017).
2 Misleading in the sense that the EU has, since the mid-1980s, integrated both non-economic as well as economic objectives within the fabric of its founding treaty framework, including notably environmental protection.
3 The first environment action programme of the (then) European Economic Community was adopted in November 1973 (OJ (1973) C112/1).
4 OJ 1987 L169. The Single European Act established the legal framework for the development of a European Union environmental policy by incorporating Title VII (Arts.130r-t) within the former European Economic Community Treaty (as subsequently superseded on 1 December 2009 by the Treaty on the Functioning of the EU (TFEU)).
5 Art.3 (3) Treaty on European Union (TEU) (OJ 2016 C202).
6 This comprises the Treaty on European Union (TEU), Treaty on the Functioning of the EU (TFEU) and the Treaty on the European Atomic Energy Community (EAEC Treaty) (consolidated versions in OJ 2016 C202). This current tripartite constitutional legal framework of the Union was established by 2007 Treaty of Lisbon (OJ 2007C306) which entered into force on 1 December 2009.
7 Article 191 Treaty on the Functioning of the EU (TFEU).
8 Art.11 TFEU.
9 OJ 2012 C83/02.
10 The EU Charter of Human Rights became a legally binding primary source of EU law by virtue of the amendments made by the 2007 Lisbon Treaty to the EU's founding treaty framework.
11 Art.37 of the EU Charter of Fundamental Rights.
12 Environment Directorate General (DGENV), European Commission: *Management Plan 2013* (Ref. ARES (2013) 416906 (14.1.2013)) at 17.
13 For some recent general commentaries on EU environmental law enforcement see e.g. Hedemann-Robinson (2017), Lenaerts/Gutiérrez-Fons (2011) and Wennerås (2007).
14 Art.17 TEU.
15 Art.19 TEU.
16 Arts.258 and 260 TFEU. By virtue of Art.259 TFEU member states of the EU also have the power to bring infringement proceedings against other member states before the CJEU, but as the case with traditional dispute settlement procedures in MEAs this facility has rarely been invoked (see e.g. Case 147/78 *France v UK* [1979] ECR I-225). For diplomatic reasons, member states prefer to defer to the European Commission (as an independent supranational institution) to supervise the application of EU law rather than become embroiled inter-state legal proceedings.

17 By virtue of the original version of the Treaty on European Union (1992 Maastricht Treaty (OJ 1992 C224)) and 2007 Lisbon Treaty (OJ 2007 C306) respectively.

18 Art.260(3) TFEU.

19 See Case C-441/17R *Commission v Poland (Puszcza Białowieska Nature Site)* EU:C:2017:877 where the CJEU held that Poland would be subject to financial penalties if it breached an interim relief order granted to the Commission under Art.279 TFEU requiring the member state to desist from forest management operations in the Puszcza Białowieska Natura 2000 site protected under the EU Habitats Directive 92/43 (OJ 1992 L206) as amended by Directive 2013/17 (OJ 2013 L158/193).

20 Art.260(2) TFEU (so-called 'second round' infringement proceedings).

21 Art.344 TFEU. The mandatory nature of EU jurisdiction was exemplified in the dispute between Ireland and the UK relating to the Sellafield mixed oxide nuclear plant: Case C-459/03 *Commission v Ireland* [2006] ECR I-4635.

22 Hedemann-Robinson (2015).

23 Specifically: Case C-387/97 *Commission v Greece (Kouroupitos landfill (2))* [1999] ECR I-3257; Case C-278/01 *Commission v Spain (Bathing Waters (2))* [2003] ECR I-14141; Case C-304/02 *Commission v France (Fishing Controls(2))* [2005] ECR I-6263; Case C-121/07 *Commission v France (GMO Controls(2))* [2008] ECR I-9195; Case C-279/11 *Commission v Ireland (EIA (2))* EU:C:2012:834; Case C-374/11 *Commission v Ireland (Waste Water Treatment Systems (2))* EU:C:2012:827;Case C-533/11 *Commission v Belgium (Waste Water Treatment Systems(2))* EU:C:2013:659; Case C-576/11*Commission v Luxembourg (Waste Water Treatment Systems(2))* EU:C:2013:773; Case C-196/13 Commission v Italy (*Italian Illegal Landfills (2))* EU:C:2014:2407; Case C-378/13 *Commission v Greece* (*Greek Illegal Landfills (2))* EU:C:2014:2405; Case C-243/13 *Commission v Sweden* (*Swedish IPPC (2))* EU:C:2014:2413; Case C-653/13*Commission v Italy (Campania Waste (2))* EU:C:2015:478; Case C-167/14 *Commission v Greece* (*Greek Urban Wastewater (2))* EU:C:2015:684; Case C-557/14 Commission v Portugal *(Portuguese Urban Wastewater (2))*EU:C:2016:471; Case C-584/14 *Commission v Greece* (*Greek Hazardous Waste Planning (2))* EU:C:2016:636 and Case C-328/16 *Commission v Greece (Thriasio Pedio Wastewater (2))* EU:C:2018:98. All CJEU judgments may be inspected online via the Court's website at: http://curia.europa.eu

24 See European Commission, *34th Annual Report of the European Commission on Monitoring the Application of Union Law (2016)* (6.7.2017) (available at: http://eur-lex.europa.eu/legal-content/EN/TXT/PDF/?uri=COM%3A2017%3A370%3AFIN&from=EN).

In the Report for 2016 the Commission notes that the environment sector represented the EU policy sector with the fourth highest number of infringement cases opened in 2016 (89 (9%)), fifth highest number of infringement cases opened in 2016 in respect of late transposition of EU directives (50 (3.5%)) and with the second highest number of unresolved cases at the end of 2016 (269 (16.2%)). Moreover, the Report recorded that in 2016 environmental cases constituted the highest number by far out of all EU policy sectors in which member states had failed to honour CJEU infringement rulings (37 (38.9%)). The environment sector constituted the fifth highest in terms of complaints from the public about alleged member state non-compliance (348 (9%)).

25 For instance, previous research by the author has revealed that environment infringement cases brought under Art.258 TFEU and concluded between 2010–2012 had taken on average 49 months for the CJEU to issue a 'first round' infringement and that on average a total of 126.5 months (10.5 years) had elapsed before the CJEU had issued a second-round judgment for cases concluded between 2010–2013: Hedemann-Robinson (2017) at 207.

26 See e.g. Jack (2011) at 75, Hedemann-Robinson (2017) at 198–203, Krämer (2003) at 381, Winter (1996) at 711.

27 See e.g. comments by Borsák (2011) at 128, Hattan (2003) at 285, Grohs (2004) at 33 and Hedemann-Robinson (2017) at 203–204.

28 See notably COM(2008)773 Commission Communication *Implementing EC Environmental Law* (18.11.2008) which clarified that infringement casework will prioritise focus on the so-called non-conformity and non-communication cases (namely cases concerning non-compliance of member state laws with EU environmental legislation)and only very serious and endemic instances of bad application (namely failures of member states to ensure practical adherence to EU environmental norms).

29 For an overview and appraisal of the impact of these legal tenets for EU environmental law enforcement purposes, see e.g. Hedemann-Robinson (2017) Chapters 6–7.

30 Case C-237/07 *Janecek v Bavaria* [2008] ECR I-6211.

31 Art.7(3) of former EU Directive 96/62 on ambient air quality assessment (OJ 1996 L296/55) as subsequently repealed and superseded by Directive 2008/50 on ambient air quality assessment and management (OJ 2008 L152/1).

32 Given that most national constitutional legal systems take the approach that norms of international law may not be relied on by individuals before national courts in the absence of national measures having transposed them into national law (dualist approach), in practice this has prevented civil society in several jurisdictions from being able to seek judicial review in respect of implementation shortcomings. In some countries, though, international environmental law has been invoked successfully before national courts: see e.g. Redgwell (2007) at 925.

33 Council Decision 2005/370 on the conclusion, on behalf of the European Community, of the Convention on access to information, public participation in decision-making and access to justice in environmental matters (OJ 2005 L124/1).

34 38 ILM 517 (1999).

35 See Art.6 of EU Directive 2003/4 on public access to environmental information (OJ 2003 L41/26).

36 Originally, the relevant access to justice provisions were contained in EU Directive 2003/35 providing for public participation in respect of the drawing up of certain plans and programmes relating to the environment and amending Directives 85/337 and 96/61 (OJ 2003 L156/17) which has been superseded by Art.11 of Directive 2011/92 on the assessment of certain public and private projects on the environment (OJ 2012 L26/1) and

Art. 25 of the recast EU Directive 2010/75 on industrial emissions (OJ 2010 L3334/17).

37 See Arts.12–13 of EU Directive 2004/35 on environmental liability (OJ 2004 L143/56).

38 EU Regulation 1367/2006 on the application of the provisions of the Århus Convention to access to information, public participation in decision-making and access to justice in environmental matters to Community institutions and bodies (OJ 2006 L264/13).

39 COM(2003)624 Commission Proposal for a Directive of the European Parliament and the Council on access to justice in environmental matters, 24.10.2003.

40 COM(2003)624 was included in the following item in the Official Journal of the EU: *Withdrawal of Obsolete Commission Proposals* (OJ 2014 C153/3).

41 See paras. 62, 65(e) and 65(v) of the Annex to EU Decision 1386/2013 on a General Union Environment Action Programme to 2020 'Living well, within the limits of our planet' (OJ 2013 L354/171).

42 As enshrined in Art.263 TFEU.

43 Named after the CJEU ruling in Case 25/62 *Plaumann v Commission* [1963] ECR 95 (see especially para 107 of judgment).

44 See notably the judgment of the CJEU in Case C-583/11P *Inuit Tapiriit Kanatami and Others* EU:C:2013:625. The CJEU held that the *Plaumann* test still applies, notwithstanding some recent treaty amendments made to Art.263 TFEU by virtue of the 2007 Lisbon Treaty.

45 Joined Cases C-401–403/12P *Council, EP and Commission v Vereniging Milieudefensie and Stichting Stop Luchtverontreiniging Utrecht*, EU: C:2015:4.

46 Report of the Compliance Committee: *Findings and recommendations with regard to communication ACCC/C/2008/32 (Part I) concerning compliance by the European Union* (ECE/MP.PP/C.1/2011/4/Add.1, 14.4.2011). For a detailed analysis of the Compliance Committee's report see e.g. Marsden (2012).

47 *Findings and recommendations of the Compliance Committee with regard to communication ACCC/C/2008/32 (Part II) concerning compliance by the European Union* (ECE/MP.PP/C.1/2017/7, 2.6.2017)

48 Art.197(1) TFEU.

49 Art.4(3) TEU.

50 EU Directive 2004/35 on environmental liability with regard to the prevention and remedying of environmental damage (OJ 2004 L143/56).

51 EU Directive 2008/99on the protection of the environment through criminal law (OJ 2008 L328/28).

52 Extensive commentary exits regarding the two instruments. On the EU Environmental liability Directive 2004/35 see for example: Betlem/Brans (2008), Hedemann-Robinson (2017) and Wilde (2013). On the EU Environmental Crimes Directive 2008/99, see for example: Cardwell/French/Hall (2011), Hedemann-Robinson (2008) and Hedemann-Robinson (2017) Chapter 13.

53 EU Directive 2003/87 establishing a scheme for greenhouse gas emission allowance trading within the Community and amending Council Directive 96/61 (OJ 2003L275/32), as amended.

54 EU Regulation 443/09 setting emission performance standards for new passenger cars as part of the Community's integrated approach to reduce CO_2 emissions from light-duty vehicles (OJ 2009 L140/1) (as amended) and EU Regulation 510/2011 setting emission performance standards for new light commercial vehicles as part of the Community's integrated approach to reduce CO_2 emissions from light-duty vehicles (OJ 2011L145/1) (as amended).
55 See Art.16 of EU Directive 2003/87 (OJ 2003 L275/32).
56 See Art.9 of EU Regulation 443/09 (OJ 2009 L140/1).
57 The EU has adopted a 'soft' non-binding general instrument: Recommendation 2001/331 providing for minimum criteria of environmental inspections in the member states (OJ 2001 L118/41).
58 The following environmental sectors now contain certain minimum inspection obligations under EU legislation: industrial emissions (EU Directive 2010/75 on industrial emissions (integrated pollution prevention and control) (recast) (OJ 2010 L334/17); major accident hazards involving dangerous substances (EU Directive 2012/18 on the control of major-accident hazards involving dangerous substances, amending and subsequently repealing Directive 96/82 (OJ 2012 L197/1) ('Seveso III')); waste management (EU Directive 2008/98 on waste and repealing certain Directives (OJ 2008 L312/ 3), EU Directive 1999/31 on the landfill of waste (OJ 1999 L182/1), EU Directive 2006/21 on the management of waste from extractive industries and amending Directive 2004/35 (OJ 2006 L102/15), EU Directive 2012/19 on waste electrical and electronic equipment (WEEE) (recast) (OJ 2012 L197/38) and EU Regulation 660/2014 amending Regulation 1013/2006 on shipments of waste 2014 O.J. (L189) 135 (EU)); ozone depleting substance management (EU Regulation 1005/2009 on substances that deplete the ozone layer (recast) (OJ 2009 L286/1)); geological storage of carbon (EU Directive 2009/31 on the geological storage of carbon dioxide and amending various Directives (OJ 2009 L140/114)); scientific experimentation on animals (Directive 2010/63 on the protection of animals used for scientific purposes (OJ 2010 L276/33)); the civil nuclear industry (Directive 2009/71 establishing a Community framework for the nuclear safety of nuclear installations (OJ 2009 L172/18) as amended by Directive 2014/87 (OJ 2014 219/42)), as well as the common fisheries policy (EU Regulation 768/2005 establishing a Community Fisheries Control Agency and amending Regulation 2847/93 (OJ 2005 L347) in conjunction with EU Regulation 1224/2009 establishing a Community control system for ensuring compliance with the rules of the Common Fisheries Policy (OJ 2009 L343)).
59 Hedemann-Robinson (2016).
60 Para. 65(iii) of the Annex to EU Decision 1386/2013 (OJ 2013 L354/171).
61 COWI, *The Costs of Not Implementing the Environmental Acquis (September 2011) – Final Report (ENV.G.1/FRA/2006/0073)* (2007). Available for inspection at: http://ec.europa.eu/environment/enveco/economics_policy/pdf/report_sept2011.pdf
62 IMPEL, *Final Report: Challenges in the Practical Implementation of EU Environmental Law and How IMPEL Could Help Overcome Them* (March 23, 2015). Available for inspection at: http://impel.eu/wp-content/uploads/2015/03/Implementation-Challenge-Report-23-March-2015.pdf

63 European Commision, *Commission Communication – Delivering the Benefits of EU Environmental Policies through a Regular Environmental Implementation Review*, 27.5.2016. See accompanying European Commission Press Release: 'New Commission environmental implementation tool could save up to €50 billion', 27.5.2016 (accessible at: http://ec.europa.eu/environment/eir/index_en.htm).

Part III

Sanctions

7 Sanctions for non-compliance in International Environmental Law

Following on from the preceding discussion, it is worth briefly taking stock of the extent to which MEAs deploy the use of sanctions as a tool for enhancing the degree of statal compliance with international environmental obligations. As generally understood, sanctions may be depicted as a means to ensure the adherence to a legal requirement or set of requirements by 'attaching a penalty to transgression'.[1] In the context of analysing enforcement of IEL, sanctions concern essentially certain measures intended to coerce or otherwise apply pressure on states, or other subjects of international law where relevant,[2] to conform to a particular internationally legally binding environmental obligation (such as the requirements binding contracting parties in a MEA's minimum environmental protection standards). They may include imposition of a penalty with a view to holding a state to account in respect of a breach of an international environmental obligation. Sanctions may be contrasted with those compliance tools and techniques intended to facilitate compliance (such as through advice, persuasion or assistance).

Overall, the use of sanctions in MEAs is relatively rare. There is a predominant preference in practice for MEA regimes to favour the use of managerialist as opposed to deterrent techniques to promote treaty compliance over the longer term where possible. Nevertheless, it is the case that coercive measures do feature in a number international environmental accords and constitute an important component of the compliance machinery and strategies used by them. MEAs may stipulate the use of sanctions against a range of targets, notably contracting parties, third parties (non-party states) or even on occasion private polluters.

The possibility of sanctions (in the broad sense of the term) being used against states as a coercive device to secure compliance is provided in some form or other in several MEAs. Notably, as discussed in Chapter 5 above, many collective non-compliance procedures established by MEAs envisage the possibility of a range of measures being used against non-compliant parties in order to bring pressure to bear on them to adhere to their treaty commitments. Typically, these range from relatively mild steps (e.g. adverse publicity via declarations of non-compliance and cautions) through to tougher measures (such as suspension of certain rights and/or treaty privileges or exceptionally the imposition of economic penalties). The latter form of measure may exert a significant degree of influence on the defaulting state, particularly where it results in the latter sustaining an adverse economic impact. This may arise in the context of some MEAs exercising some degree of control over transboundary trade. Accordingly, a decision to suspend the right to trade in certain species under the aegis of CITES[3] may prove economically damaging to exporter countries. A failure to comply with carbon emission reduction targets under the 1997 Kyoto Protocol[4] may attract a penalty in the form of significant additional carbon emissions reductions obligations resulting in additional compliance costs.[5] By way of complement to sanctions that may be imposed by non-compliance procedures in MEAs, general principles of international law concerning the imposition of counter-measures underscore the traditional dispute resolution procedures contained in international environmental accords (as discussed in Chapter 4 above).

Beyond the limited range of sanctions that may be applied to contracting parties in international law and practice, some MEAs also provide for coercive measures to be imposed on non-parties as a means of upholding the integrity of the international environmental pact. A notable example is the 1987 Montreal Protocol.[6] Specifically, Article 4 of the Protocol requires contracting parties to desist from engaging in trade in controlled ozone depleting substances with non-parties which do not adhere to the minimum requirements set down in the international agreement. Similar types of restrictions are contained in the 1973 Convention on International Trade in Endangered Species (CITES), the 1989 UN Basel Convention, 2000 Cartagena Biosafety Protocol and the 2001 UN Stockholm Convention on Persistent Organic Pollutants (POPs).[7] Other MEAs, such as those focusing on the conservation of fisheries, allow for the possibility of contracting parties deploying trade-related sanctions against non-party states whose vessels are found to engage in illegal or unregulated fishing in an area covered by the fisheries agreement.[8] The compatibility between this type of MEA restriction and World Trade Organisation (WTO) obligations has never been formally tested or clarified, and it remains a moot point as to whether they may be justified as an acceptable defence within the parameters of WTO rules.[9]

Finally, some MEAs may make provision for sanctions of various kinds to be targeted at individual polluters. In general, for reasons associated with statal sensitivities over national sovereignty, few international accords require contracting parties to introduce punitive measures to be imposed on individuals acting in breach of minimum treaty requirements. Nevertheless, a handful of MEAs include some stipulations on the subject of national level enforcement mechanisms. Only very few MEAs require contracting parties to ensure that their criminal laws include provision for the punishment of individual conduct that contravenes treaty obligations, notably these being CITES, the UN Basel Convention and the EU.[10] As far as civil liability is concerned, a few MEAs require contracting parties to ensure that arrangements are in place to ensure that polluters are required to pay compensation in respect of environmental damage. To date, these include MEAs on civil liability concerning the civil nuclear sector and oil pollution from ships[11]. In addition, as noted in Chapter 6, the European Union has adopted a legislative instrument on environmental liability[12] requiring national authorities to hold persons responsible for environmental damage to account.

Notes

1 *The Shorter Oxford English Dictionary* 6th ed (Oxford UP, 2007) Vol. I at 833 and Vol. II at 2661 respectively.
2 Such as a regional international organisation party to an MEA, such as the European Union.
3 983 U.N.T.S. 243 (1973).
4 37 ILM 22 (1998).
5 See Para. XV of Decision 24/CP.7.
6 26 ILM 154 (1987).
7 Specifically: Art.X of CITES; Art.4(5) in conjunction with Art. 11 of the 1989 UN Basel Convention (28 ILM 657 (1989)); Art.24 of the 2000 Biosafety Protocol (39 ILM 1027 (2000)); and Art.3(2)(b)(iii)of the UN Stockholm Convention on POPs (40 ILM 532 (2001)).
8 See e.g. Art.20(7) of the 1995 UN Straddling Fish Stocks Agreement (34 ILM 1542 (1995)).
9 Specifically, whether justified under Article XX of the 1994 General Agreement on Tariffs and Trade (GATT) (LT/UR/A-1A/9). See e.g. comments by Birnie/Boyle/Redgwell (2009) at 766–769, Sands/Peel (2018) at 843–847.
10 These include notably: Art.9 of the 1989 UN Basel Convention (28 ILM 657 (1989)); Art. VIII of CITES; the 1998 Council of Europe Convention on Environmental Crime (1998 C.E.T.S.72) (not yet in force) and the EU's Environmental Crimes Directive 2008/99 (OJ 2008 L328/28).
11 Namely, the 1960 Paris OECD Convention on Third Party Liability in the Field of Nuclear Energy (956 U.N.T.S. 251), 1963 IAEA Vienna

Convention on Civil Liability for Nuclear Damage (1063 U.N.T.S. 265), 1992 International Convention on Civil Liability for Oil Pollution Damage (IMO LEG/CONF.9/15), 1992 and 2003 Protocols to the Brussels Convention on the Establishment of an International Fund for Compensation of Oil Pollution Damage (BNA 21: 1751 and 92FUND/A.8/4 respectively) and the 2001 Convention on Civil Liability for Bunker Oil Pollution Damage (40 ILM 1493 (2001)). For an overview and appraisal of MEA developments on environmental civil liability, see e.g. Sands/Peel (2018) at 771–804.

12 EU Directive 2004/35 (OJ 2004 L143/56).

Part IV

Reflections on international enforcement of International Environmental Law

8 Concluding remarks

Notwithstanding recent innovations at international level within MEA regimes to promote collective compliance procedures and tools for the purpose of assisting in enhancing the degree of adherence by states to their international environmental obligations, it is clear that the field of IEL concerning enforcement and sanctions is underdeveloped and fragmented. A pre-eminent role is effectively given to states under general tenets of international law in overseeing the development and implementation of international rules of law. Most states maintain a clear and firm preference to maintain, as far as possible, exclusive sovereign control in respect of anthropogenic activities carried out within their respective individual territories. As a consequence, the enforcement of international environmental protection obligations has been largely dependent upon the effectiveness of national rules of law and statal administrative resources and systems in order to oversee their proper application. States have, on the whole, been reluctant to cede control and/or oversight to independent supranational institutions for the purpose of overseeing due application of internationally binding environmental protection rules. The development of such compliance control systems has been a gradual, patchy and generally hard-fought affair in the context of international negotiations over MEA building with genuinely global dimensions.

However, it would be incorrect to dismiss or ignore the actual and potential influence that international legal principles and procedures may bring to bear on states to respect their basic duty to adhere to international environmental obligations. As highlighted in this book, a number of compliance mechanisms and tools of a formal as well as informal nature have become woven into contemporary framework of IEL which undoubtedly exert a degree of influence on states' observance of their international environmental obligations. The classic international principle of state responsibility, without doubt a cornerstone tenet of contemporary IEL, remains highly relevant in assisting the resolution of disputes between states over instances of actual or potential transboundary environmental damage perpetrated by one state with adverse environmental impacts on another. The inclusion of inter-state dispute resolution clauses within most MEAs, now standard practice, also exerts influence on states to refrain from breaching MEAs that might or in fact lead to significant damage to the treaty rights of certain other contracting parties.

Above all, the development of collective compliance control mechanisms, particularly crystallised in the form of non-compliance procedures that have emerged within several MEAs since the early 1990s, has been a welcome and much needed complement to the traditional bilateral inter-statal dispute resolution machinery. For non-compliance procedures are far better suited than inter-statal dispute resolution systems to addressing collective environmental protection problems and interests. Moreover, the facilitative and non-adversarial nature and context-sensitive approach of non-compliance procedures constitute attractive qualities from an IEL enforcement perspective. Their collaborative nature, by aiming to avoid blame and punishment of individual defaulting contracting parties to an international environmental accord, reflects a realistic strategy to provide a pathway to enhancing long-term compliance with MEA objectives.

The brutal reality is that states retain power to determine the extent of environmental ambition in MEAs and to decide whether to accede to or withdraw from such international co-operation. In addition, they have shown a general marked reluctance to agree to endow treaty bodies with strong supervisory or sanctioning powers for the purpose of assisting in MEA enforcement-related activities. Only very rarely have states agreed to subscribe to international institutional mechanisms of law enforcement foreseeing the imposition of penalties in respect of breaches of MEA regimes, reflective of a deterrent approach (such as the EU and the 1997 Kyoto Protocol). The reality of hegemonic statal power relationships and dynamics is also reflected in the relatively soft range of response measures contemplated even for relatively sophisticated non-compliance procedural systems such as the one deployed under the aegis of the 1987 Montreal Protocol. In practice, sanctions such as cautions and suspension of treaty rights have only been used very rarely and as last resort options in the face of persistent offending.

International compliance mechanisms are ultimately crucial for law enforcement purposes precisely because undue reliance on nation states to implement their MEA obligations runs a serious risk that MEA objectives of tackling serious regional and global environmental problems may be significantly weakened, hampered or even defeated. Whilst the international community has invested considerable efforts into encouraging states to ensure that their national legal and administrative systems are appropriately equipped to implement MEA requirements, such as through the work and efforts of bodies such as UNEP,[1] assumptions made about the diligence of states (in the long-term) to honour their obligations is ultimately an inadequate and risky strategy to pursue. Without doubt the concept of collective non-compliance mechanisms in MEA regimes constitutes a major breakthrough for the purposes of enhancing statal compliance. However, to date the quality of non-compliance procedures across MEAs has been patchy and uncoordinated. Relatively few non-compliance procedures dispose of a sufficiently broad range of tools and measures akin to that established for the Montreal Protocol, and some MEAs which contain notable environmental protection obligations still do not include any collective non-compliance mechanism.[2]

The current state of affairs position reflects a general lack of political will amongst states to prioritise and engage in supporting and following up initiatives to review the relative effectiveness of compliance control mechanisms in existence across the spectrum of international environmental agreements. In entrusting an informal intergovernmental body (the so-called High Level Political Forum) as opposed to an independent international organ (e.g. UNEP) with the task of following up on the implementation of sustainable development, the outcome of the 2012 Rio + 20 UN Conference[3] exemplified the marked degree of reluctance shared by most states to invest in taking substantial measures to enhance systems of international environmental governance. On account of the relative low political priority attached by governments generally to IEL implementation issues, it is not that surprising to find that progress on developing a more coherent and co-ordinated system of non-compliance procedural structures amongst MEAs has been pretty slow.[4] Some useful efforts have been made amongst certain MEA regimes to promote synergies[5] as well as exchange experience and best practice regarding addressing non-compliance issues.[6] However, there is crucially an absence of clear and definitive political leadership and appetite currently over securing the future effective development of international collective compliance of IEL. Until that state of affairs is rectified, we are most likely to witness a continuation of rather anaemic and haphazard progress of efforts made at international level to bolster efforts to improve upon the state of enforcement of IEL.

Notes

1 For example, under the aegis of the (currently fourth) Montevideo Programme (http://www.unep.org/delc/EnvironmentalLaw/tabid/54403/Default.aspx) and other initiatives such as the declaration adopted at the 2002 Global Judges Symposium on Sustainable Development and the Role of Law, available at: http://www.unep.org/Documents.Multilingual/Default.asp?ArticleID=3115&DocumentID=259.
2 Examples include the 1971 Ramsar Convention (996 U.N.T.S. 245), 1946 International Whaling Convention (161 U.N.T.S. 72), 1972 London Marine Dumping Convention (1046 U.N.T.S. 120) and 1979 Bonn Convention (19 ILM 15 (1980)).
3 See paras. 84–86 of the political outcome document of the UN Conference *The Future We Want*, as endorsed by the UN General Assembly in Resolution 66/288 of 27.7.2012 (A/RES/66/288) available at: https://sustainabledevelopment.un.org/index.php?menu=1298.
4 For example, discussions over prospective non-compliance procedural mechanisms within the 1998 Rotterdam Convention (38 ILM 1 (1998)) and 2001 Stockholm Convention (40 ILM 532 (2001)) have been unresolved for several years now (since 2005).
5 For instance, in the chemicals sectors between the 1989 Basel Convention (28 ILM 657 (1989)), 1998 Rotterdam Convention (*supra* note 4) and 2001 Stockholm Convention (*supra* note 4).
6 See e.g. para. IV.A.4 of the *Report of the 10th Meeting of the Basel Convention Implementation and Compliance Committee* (UNEP/CHW/CC.10/14, 5–6.12.2013) which notes a dialogue with compliance bodies of other MEAs in the context of a review to enhance timely and complete national reporting.

Bibliography

AdsettH, DanielA, HusainM, McDormanT, 'Compliance Committees and Recent Multilateral Environmental Agreements: The Canadian Experience and Their Negotiation and Operation' (2004) 42*Can Ybk of Internat Law* 91

AntonD K, '"Treaty congestion" in contemporary International Environmental Law' in ShawkatA, BhuiyanJ H, ChowdhuryT M R, TecheraE J (eds), *Routledge Handbook of International Environmental Law* (Routledge, 2013)

BeckerG, 'Crime and Punishment: An Economic Approach' (1968) 76(2) *J of Polit Econ* 169

BellS, McGillivrayD, PedersenO, *Environmental Law*9th ed (OUP, 2017)

BetlemG, BransE (eds), *Environmental Liability in the EU: The 2004 Directive Compared with the US and Member State Law* (Cameron May, 2008)

BiniazS, 'Remarks about the CITES Compliance Regime' in BeyerlinU, StollP-T, WolfrumR (eds) *Ensuring Compliance with Multilateral Environmental Agreements: A Dialogue Between Practitioners and Academia* (Martinus Nijhoff, 2006)

BirnieP, BoyleA, RedgwellC, *International law and the Environment*3rd ed (Cambridge UP, 2009)

BodanskyD, *The Art and Craft of International Environmental Law* (Harvard UP, 2010)

BorsákL, *The Impact of Environmental Concerns on the Public Enforcement Mechanism under EU Law: Environmental Protection in the 25th Hour* (Kluwer, 2011)

BoyleA, 'Saving the World? Implementation and Enforcement of International Environmental Law through International Institutions' (1991) 3*JEL* 229

Brown WeissE, JacobsonH (eds), *Engaging Countries: Strengthening Compliance with International Environmental Accords* (MIT Press, 2000)

BrownlieI, *Principles of Public International Law*4th ed (Oxford1990)

BrunnéeJ, 'Enforcement Mechanisms in International Law and International Environmental Law' (2005) 1*ELNI Review* 1

Cardesa-SalzmannA, 'Constitutionalising Secondary Rules in Global Environmental Regimes: Non-Compliance Procedures and the Enforcement of Multilateral Environmental Agreements' (2011) 24(1)*JEL* 103

CardwellP, FrenchD, HallM, 'Tackling Environmental Crime in the EU: The Case of the Missing Victim?' (2011) 1*Env'l Liability* 35
ChayesA, ChayesA H, 'On Compliance' (1993) 47(2)*International Organisation* 175
CITES Interpretation and Implementation of the Convention: Compliance and Enforcement, Convention on International Trade in Endangered Species (2013), Sixteenth Meeting of the Conference of the Parties (Bangkok), COP-16 Doc.28. Available at: https://www.cites.org/sites/default/files/eng/cop/16/doc/E-CoP16-28.pdf
COWI, 'The Costs of Not Implementing the Environmental Acquis (September 2011) - Final Report (ENV.G.1/FRA/2006/0073)' (2011). Available at: http://ec.europa.eu/environment/enveco/economics_policy/pdf/report_sept2011.pdf
De WitteB, 'EU Law: Is It International Law?' (Chapter 7) in BarnardC, PeersS (eds), *European Union Law*2nd ed (OUP, 2017)
DownsG W, RockeD M, BarsoomP N, 'Is the Good News about Compliance Good News about Co-Operation?' (1996) 50*International Organisation* 379
DupuyP-M, VinualesJ E , *International Environmental Law* (Cambridge UP, 2015)
FitzmauriceM, RedgwellC, 'Environmental Non-Compliance Procedures and International Law' (2000) *Netherlands Yrbk Internat Law* 35
GoetynN, MaesF, 'Compliance Mechanisms in MEAs: An Effective Way to Compliance?' (2011) 10*Chinese Jl Intern Law* 791
GrohsS, 'Commission Infringement Procedure in Environment Cases' in OnidaM (ed) *Europe and the Environment: Legal Essays in Honour of Ludwig Krämer* (Europa Law Publishing, 2004)
HattanE, 'The Implementation of EU Environmental Law' (2003) 15(3) *JEL* 273
Hedemann-RobinsonM, 'The Emergence of European Union Environmental Criminal Law: A Quest for Solid Foundations: Parts I and II' (2008) 16(3) *Env' Liability* 71 and 16(3) *Env' Liability* 111
Hedemann-RobinsonM, 'Enforcement of EU Environmental Law: Taking Stock of the Evolving Union Legal Framework' (2015) 24*EEELR* 115
Hedemann-RobinsonM, 'Environmental Inspections and the EU: Securing an Effective Role for a Supranational Union Legal Framework' (2016) 6(1) *Transnational Env'l Law Jl* 1–28. DOI: doi:10.1017/S2047102515000291. Available at: http://journals.cambridge.org/abstract_S2047102515000291
Hedemann-RobinsonM, *Enforcement of European Union Environmental Law: Legal Issues and Challenges*2nd ed (Routledge 2017, as updated from 2015)
HunterD, SalzmanJ, ZaelkeD , *International Environmental Law and Policy*4th ed (2011)
IMPEL (European Network for the Implementation and Enforcement of Environmental Law), Final Report: Challenges in the Practical Implementation of EU Environmental Law and How IMPEL Could Help Overcome Them, March 23, 2015. Available at: http://impel.eu/wp-content/uploads/2015/07/Implementation-Challenge-Report-23-March-2015.pdf

JackB, 'Enforcing Member State Compliance with EU Environmental Law: A Critical Evaluation of the Use of Financial Penalties' (2011) 23(1) *JEL* 73

JendrośkaJ, 'Aarhus Convention Compliance Committee: Origins, Status and Activities' (2011) 8(4) *JEEPL* 301

KlabbersJ, 'Compliance Procedures' in BodanskyD, BrunnéeJ, HeyE, *Oxford Handbook on International Environmental Law* (OUP, 2007)

KoesterV, 'The Compliance Committee of the Aarhus Convention: An Overview of Procedures and Jurisprudence' (2007) 37(2–3) *Environmental Policy and Law* 83

KrämerL, *EC Environmental Law*5th ed (Sweet & Maxwell, 2003)

KrämerL (ed), *Enforcement of Environmental Law* (E Elgar, 2016)

KravchenkoS, 'The Aarhus Convention and Innovations in Compliance with Multilateral Environmental Law and Policy' (2007) 18(1) *Colorado Jl of International Environmental Law and Policy* 1

LenaertsK, Gutiérrez-FonsJ A, 'The General System of EU Environmental Law Enforcement' (2011) 30(1) *Ybk of European Law* 3

Malmö Ministerial Declaration, Governing Council of UNEP, (2000) Global Ministerial Environment Forum, 6th Spec. Sess., 5th Plenary Meeting. Available at: https://unep.ch/natcom/assets/milestones/malmo_declaration.PDF

MarauhnT, 'Towards a Procedural Law of Compliance Control in International Environmental Relations' (1996) *Zeitschrift für Ausländisches, Öffentliches und Völkerrecht* 707

MarsdenS, 'Direct Public Access to EU Courts: Upholding Public International Law via the Aarhus Convention Compliance Committee' (2012) 81*Nordic Jl of Internat. Law* 175

MitchellR B, 'Compliance Theory: Compliance, Effectiveness and Behaviour Change in International Environmental Law' in BodanskyD, BrunnéeJ, HeyE, *Oxford Handbook on International Environmental Law* (OUP, 2007)

NeumayerE, Multilateral Environmental Agreements, Trade and Development: Issues and Policy Options concerning Compliance and Enforcement (2012) LSE Research Online paper – Report for the Consumer Unity and Trust Society (Jaipur, India). Available at: http://www.lse.ac.uk/geographyAndEnvironment/whosWho/profiles/neumayer/pdf/CUTS.pdf

O'ConnellM E, 'Enforcement and the Success of International Environmental Law' (1995–1996) 3*Indiana Jl of Global Legal Studies* 47

PallemaertsM (ed), *The Aarhus Convention at Ten: Interactions and Tensions between Conventional International Law and EU Environmental Law* (Europa Verlag, 2011)

PeelJ, 'New State Responsibility Rules and Compliance with Multilateral Environmental Obligations: Some Case Studies of How the New Rules Might Apply in the Environmental Context' (2001) 10(1) *RECIEL* 82

RedgwellC, 'National Implementation' in BodanskyD, BrunnéeJ, HeyE, *Oxford Handbook on International Environmental Law* (OUP, 2007)

RinceneauJ, 'Enforcement Mechanisms in International Environmental Law: Quo Vadunt?' (2000) 15*Jl Env Law and Litigation* 147

RomanoC P R, 'International Dispute Settlement' in BodanskyD, BrunnéeJ, HeyE, *Oxford Handbook on International Environmental Law* (OUP, 2007)

SandP H, 'Enforcing CITES: The Rise and Fall of Trade Sanctions' (2013) 22 (3) *RECIEL* 251

SandsP, 'Non-compliance and Dispute Settlement' in BeyerlinU, StollP-T, WolfrumR (eds) *Ensuring Compliance with Multilateral Environmental Agreements: A Dialogue Between Practitioners and Academia* (Martinus Nijhoff, 2006)

SandsP, PeelJ, *Principles of International Environmental Law*4th ed (Cambridge UP, 2018)

SolomonS, IvyD J, KinnisonD, MillsM J, Neely III R J, SchmidtA, 'Emergence of Healing in the Antarctic Ozone Layer' (2016) 353(6296) *Science* 269

ThirlwayH, 'The Sources of International Law' in EvansM D (ed), *International Law* (OUP, 2003)

UNECE, *Guidelines for Strengthening Compliance and Implementation of Multilateral Environmental Agreements in the ECE Region* (ECE/CEP/107 as adopted by the Fifth UNECE Ministerial Conference Environment for Europe, Kiev, 21–23. 5. 2003), (UNECE, 2003).

UNEP, *Guidelines on Compliance and Enforcement of Multilateral Environmental Agreements* (UNEP, 2002)

UNEP, *Compliance Mechanisms Under Selected Multilateral Agreements* (UNEP, 2007)

UNEP, *The Basel Mechanism for Promoting Implementation and Compliance: Celebrating a Decade of Assistance to Parties* (UNEP, 2011)

UNEP, GEO5 *Global Environment Outlook: Environment for the Future We Want* (2012) at 464. Available at: http://www.unep.org/geo/geo5.asp

United Nations, *Charter of the United Nations*, 24 October 1945, 1 UNTS XVI. Available at: http://www.un.org/en/sections/un-charter/un-charter-full-text/

VidalJ, 'Many Treaties to Save the Earth, but Where's the Will to Implement Them?' in *The Guardian* newspaper (7.6.2012). Available at: https://www.theguardian.com/environment/blog/2012/jun/07/earth-treaties-environmental-agreements

WenneråsP, *The Enforcement of EC Environmental Law* (Oxford, 2007)

WettestadJ, 'Monitoring and Verification' Settlement' in BodanskyD, BrunnéeJ, HeyE, *Oxford Handbook on International Environmental Law* (OUP, 2007)

WildeM, *Civil Liability for Environmental Damage: Comparative Analysis of Law and Policy in Europe and the US*2nd ed (Kluwer, 2013)

WinterG, 'On the Effectiveness of the EC Administration: The Case of Environmental Protection' (1996) 33*CMLRev* 689

YoshidaO, 'Procedural Aspects of the International Legal Regime for Climate Change: Early Operation of the Kyoto Protocol's Compliance System' (2011) 4*Jl of East Asia & Internat. Law* 41

ZaelkeD, HigdonT, 'The Role of Compliance in the Rule of Law, Good Governance and Sustainable Development' (2006) 5*JEEPL* 383

Index